F!FTY DOORS OF

KiSS MY ASS

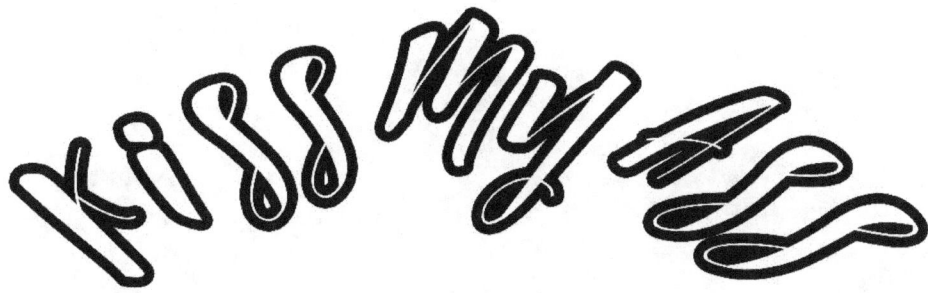

40 Swear Words to Color

For Stress Releasing

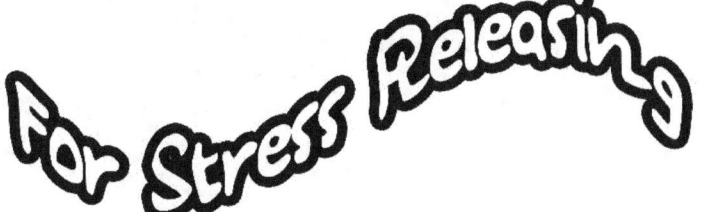

BY

J.A. FLORENTINE

Happy Coloring!

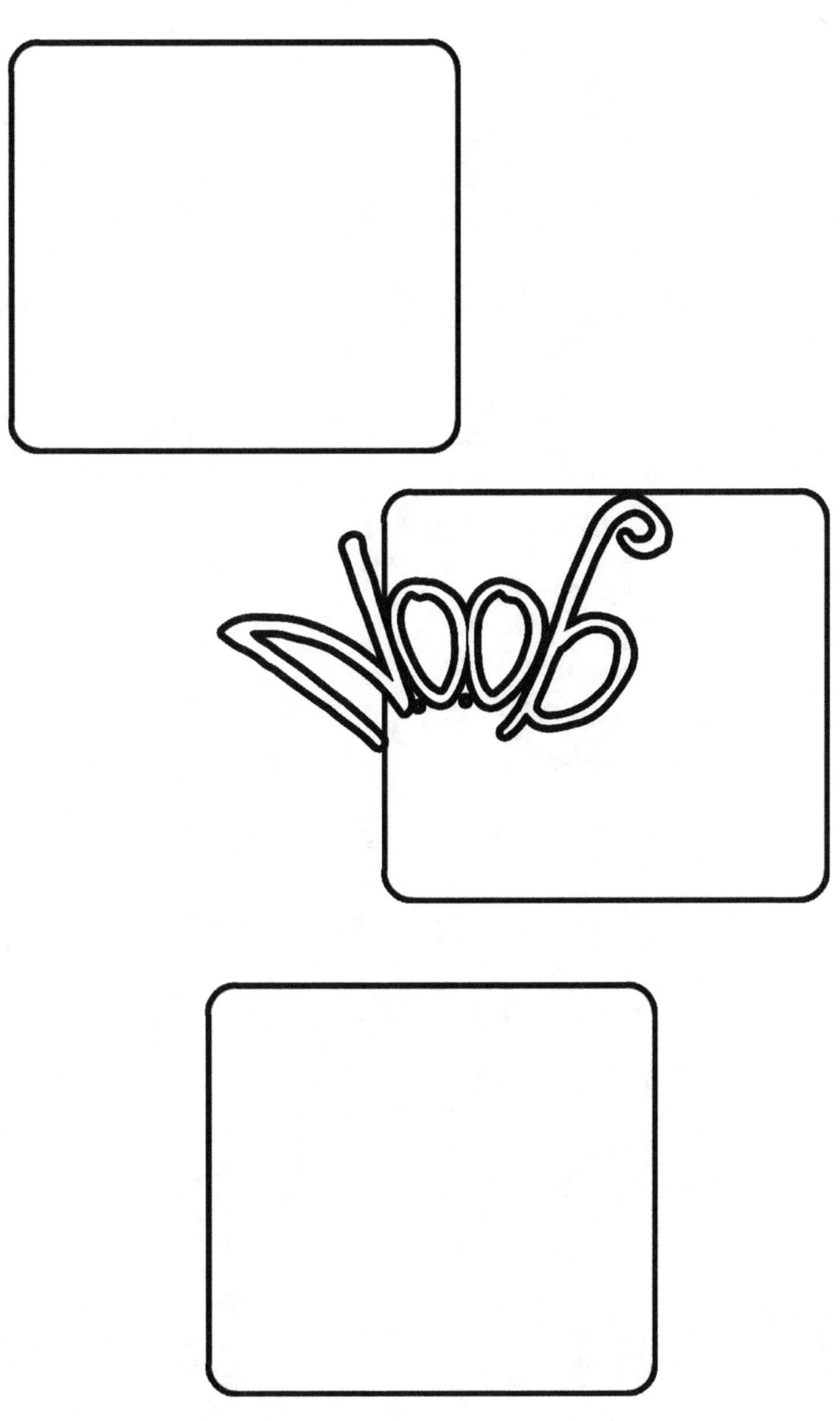

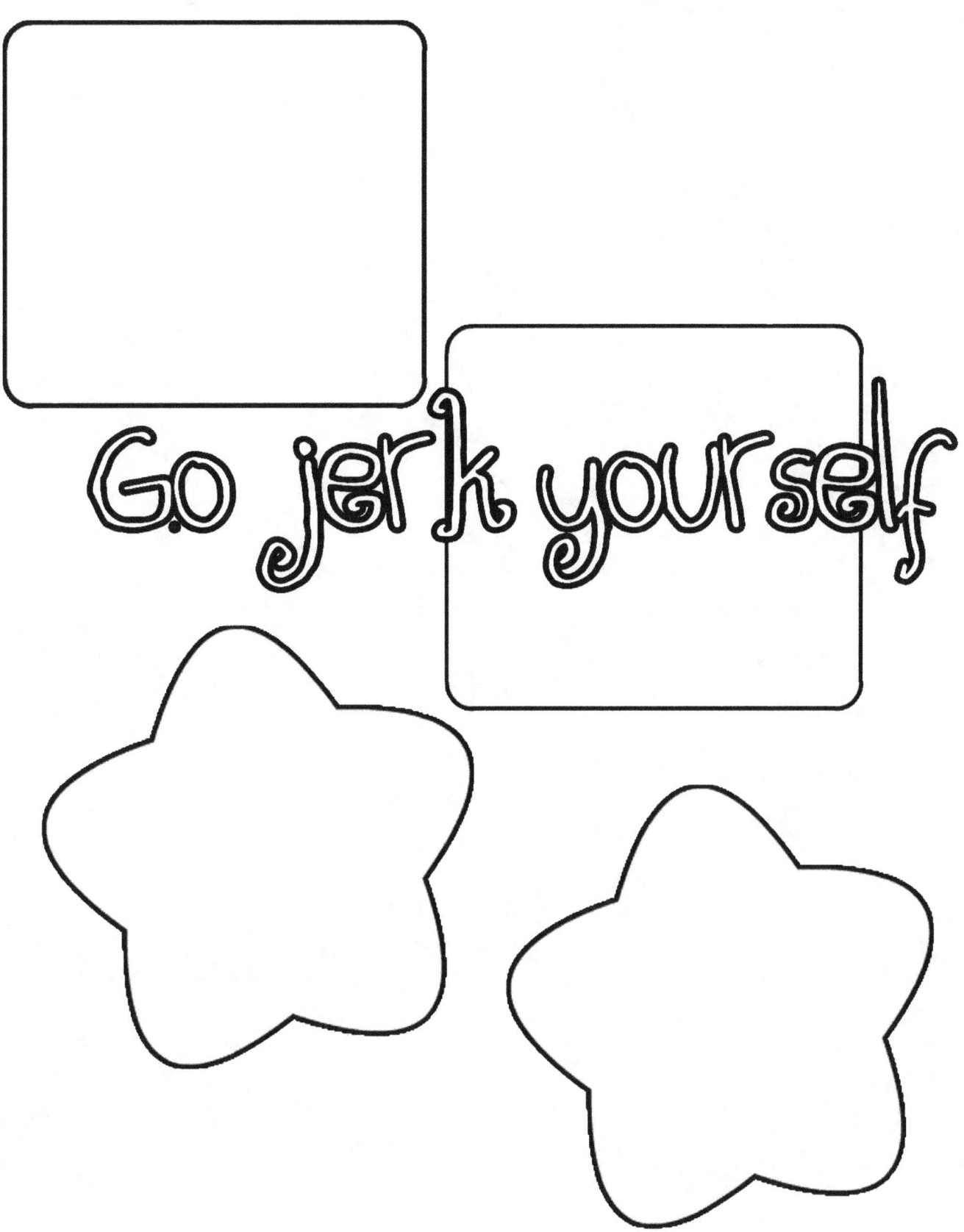

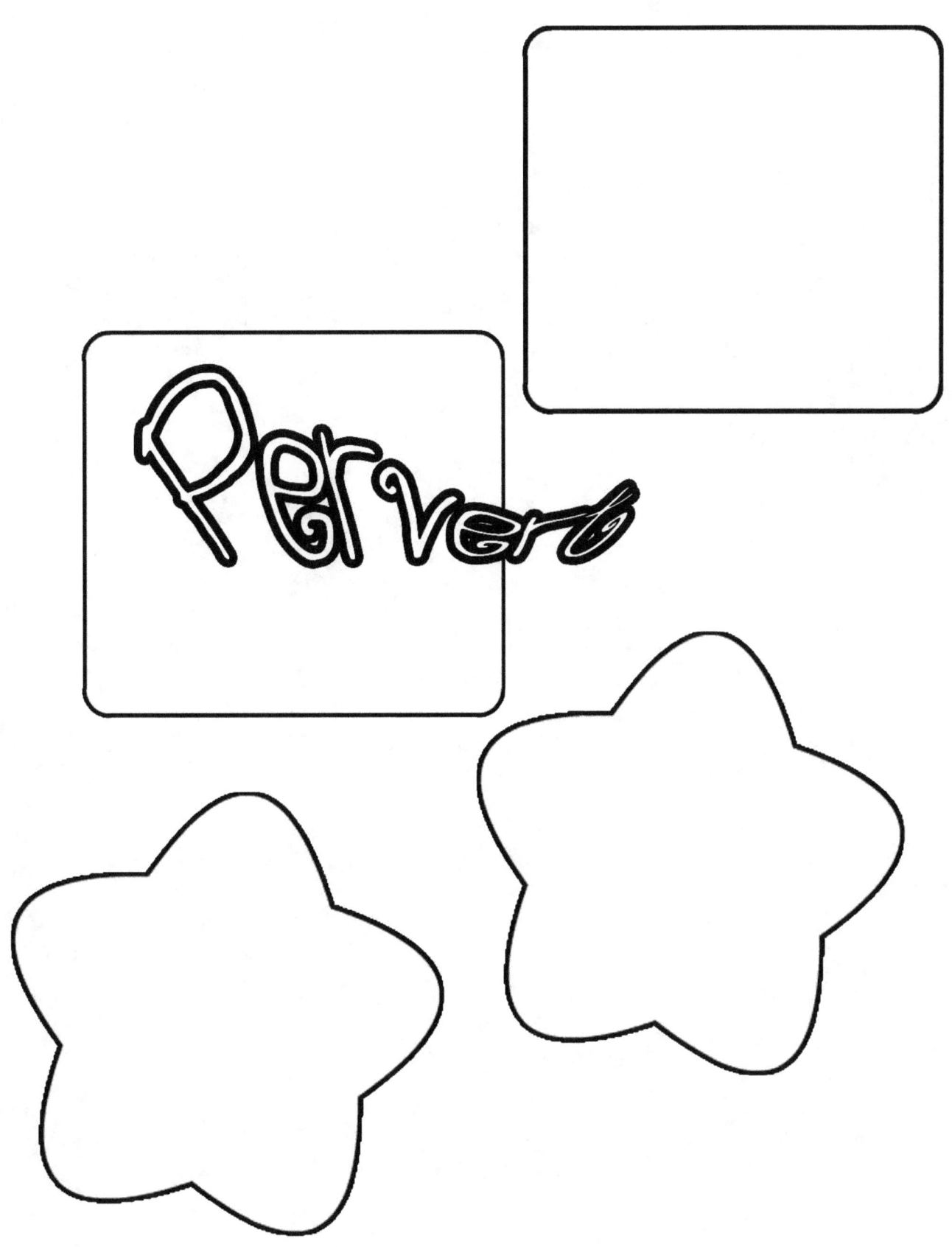

Attention Whore

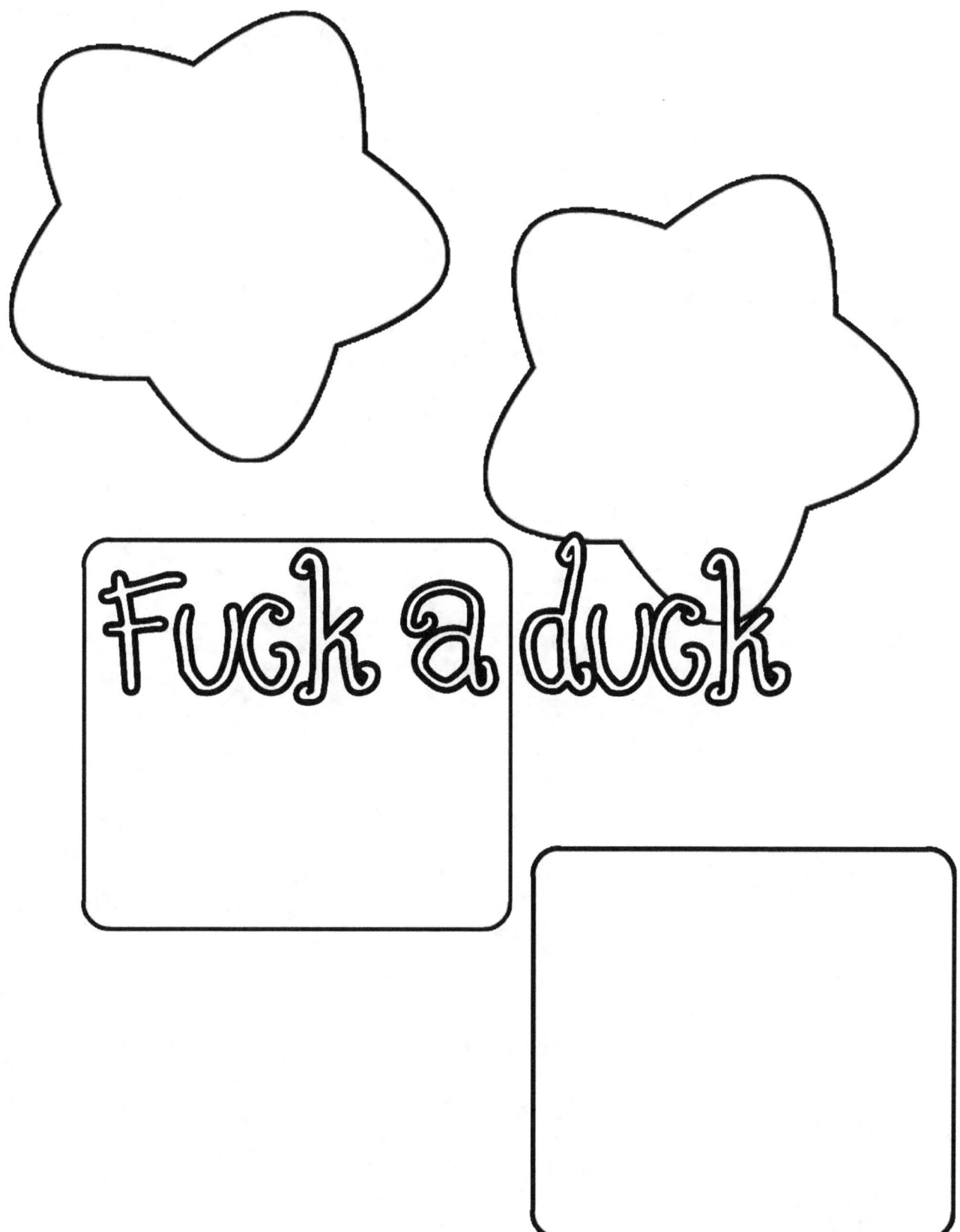

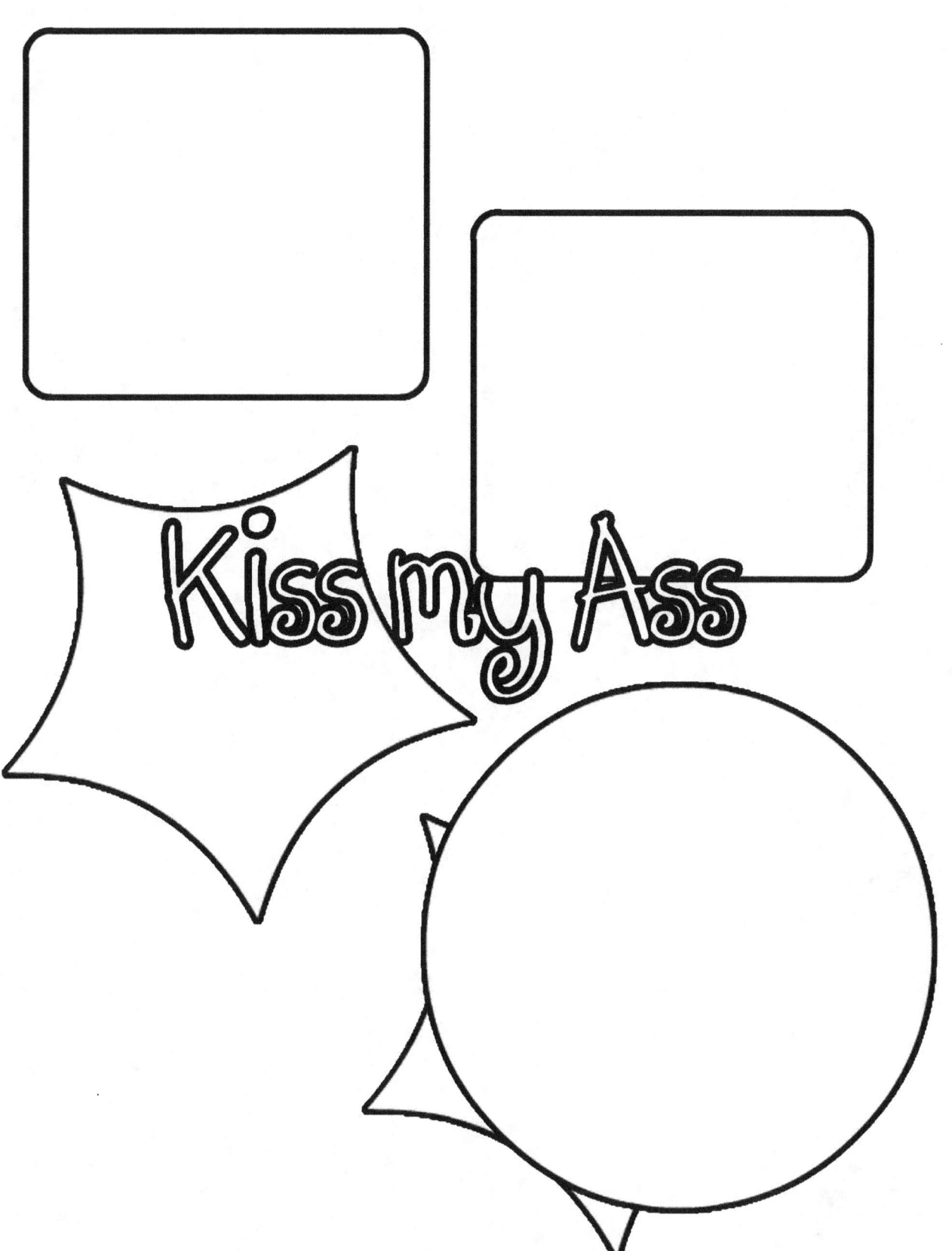

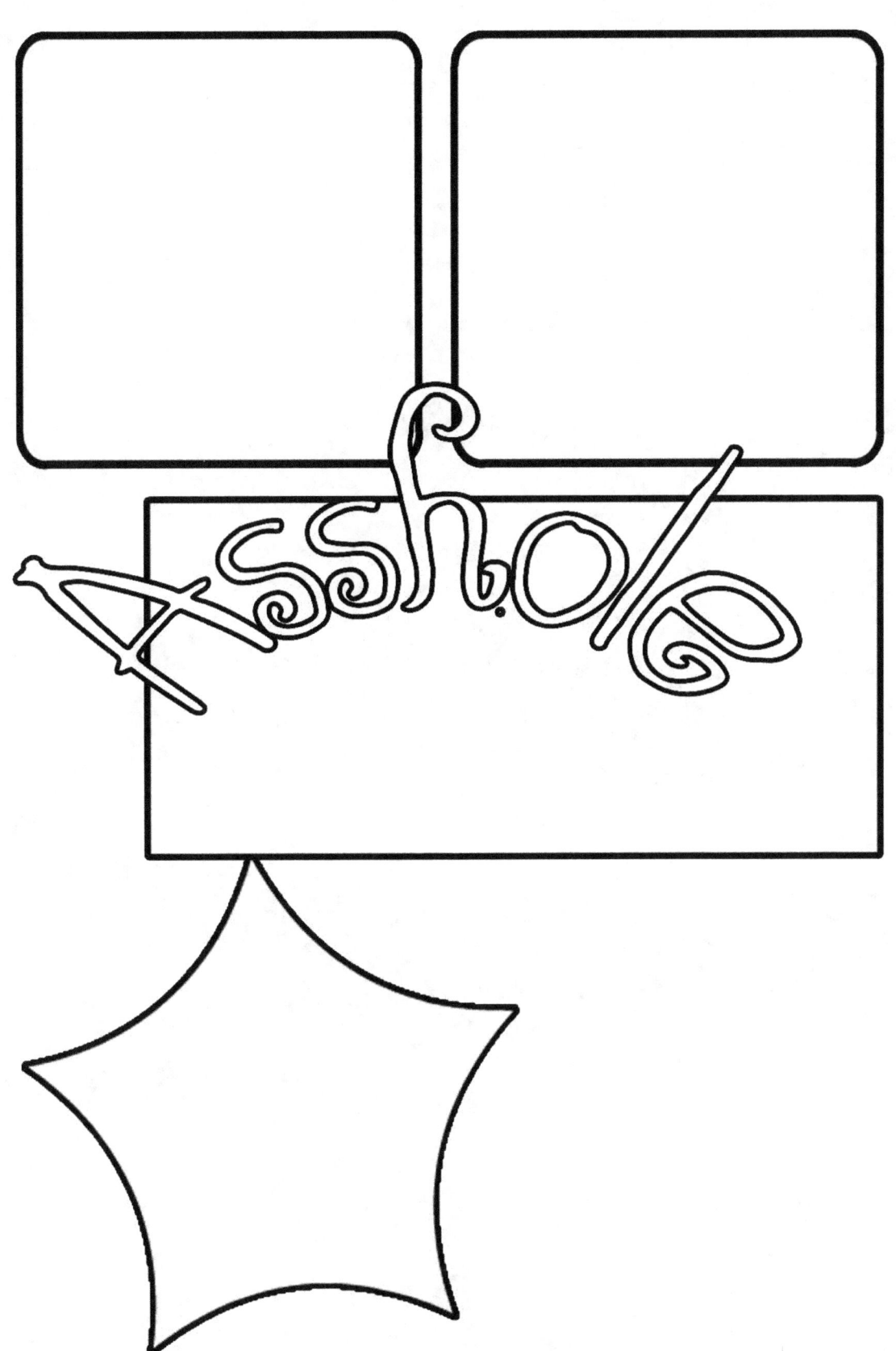

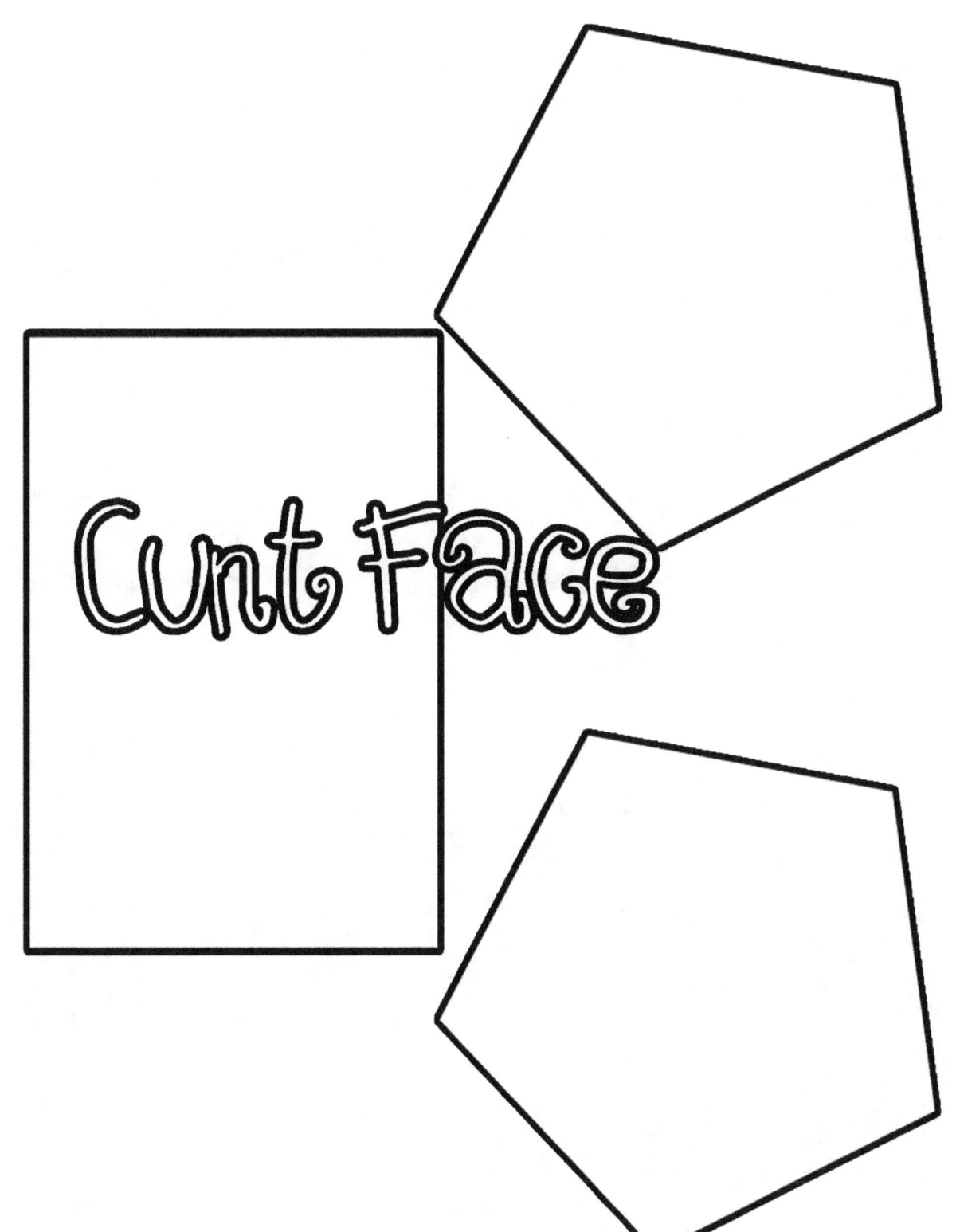

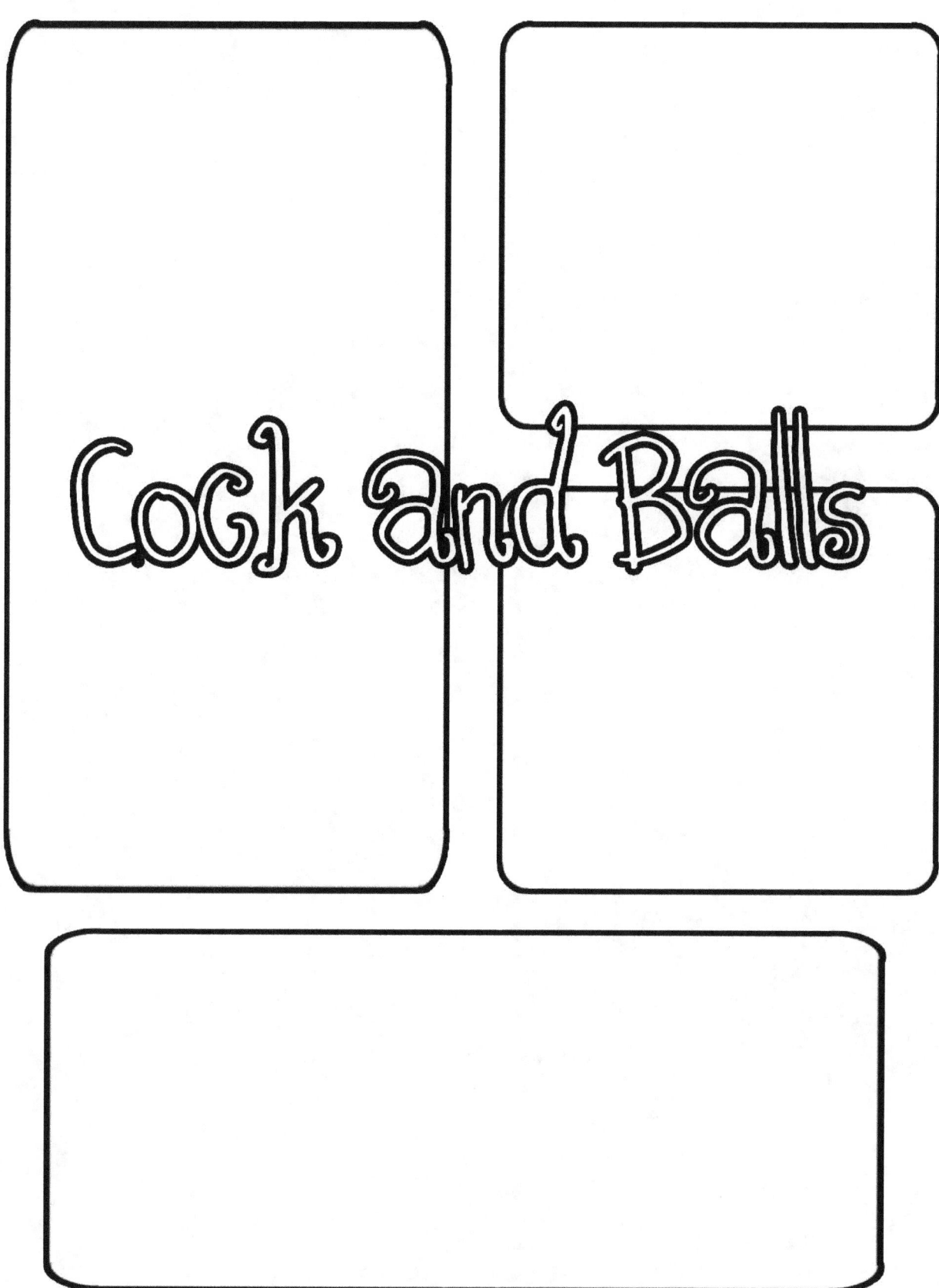

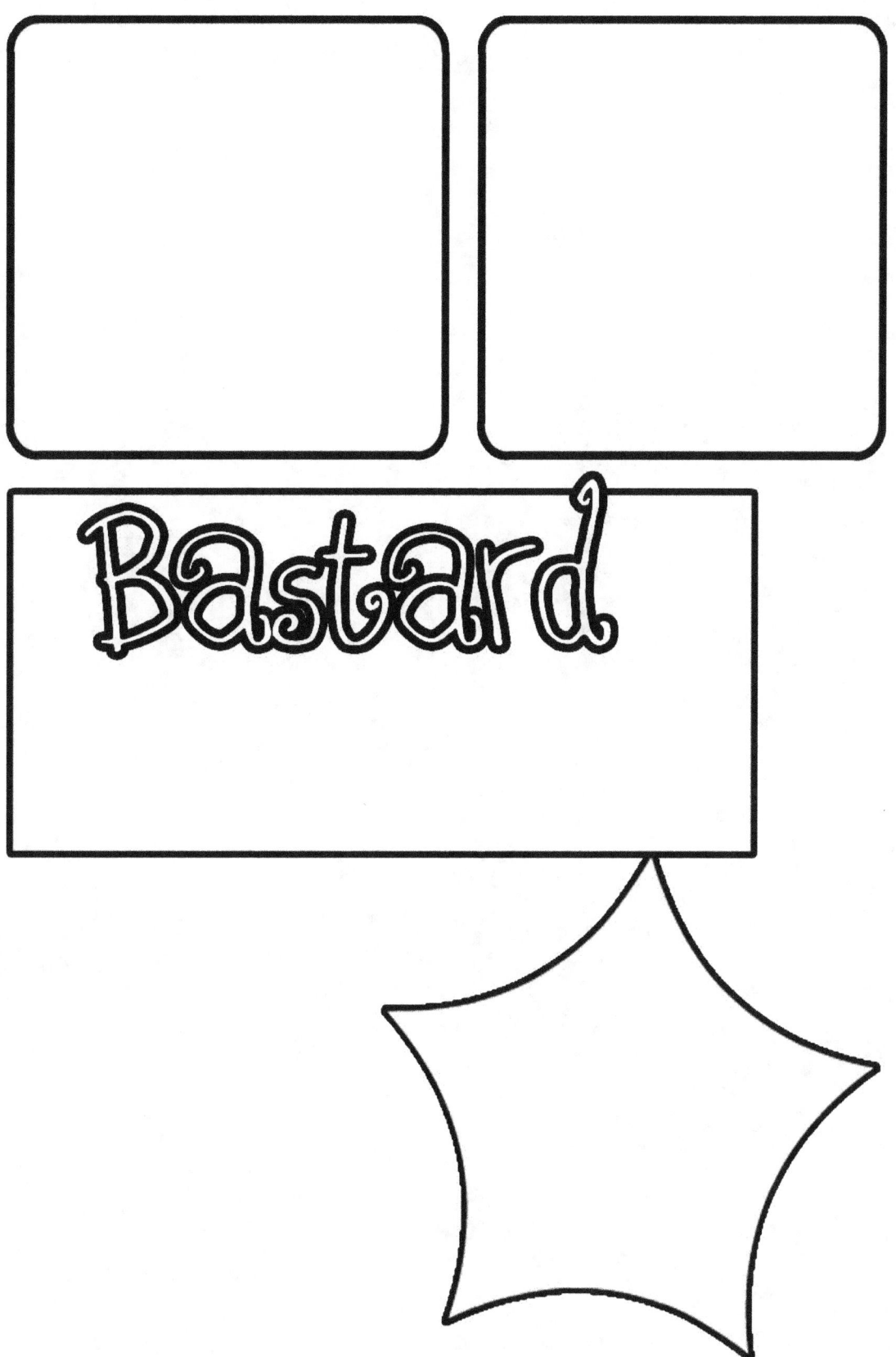

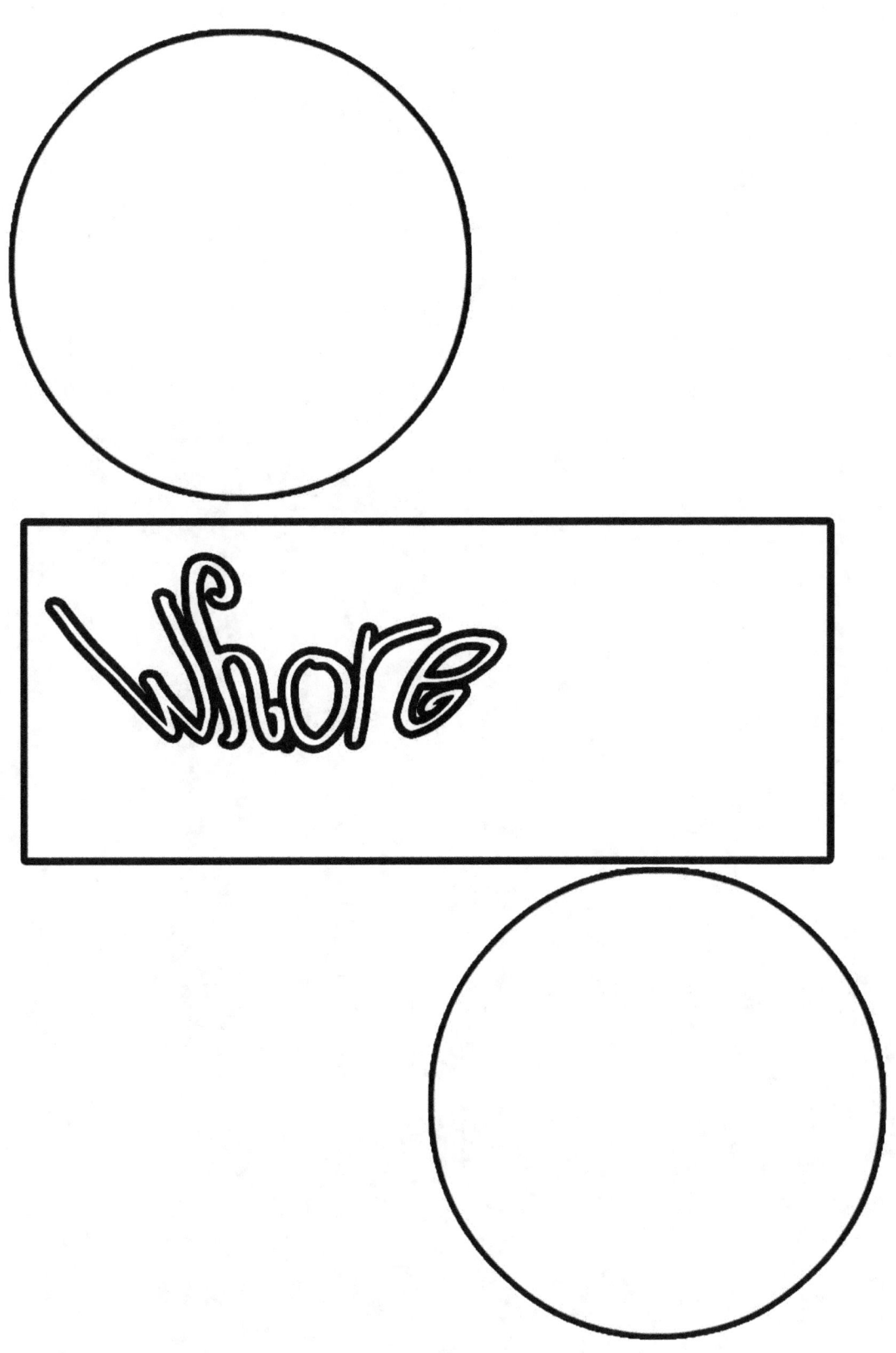

Batshit Crazy

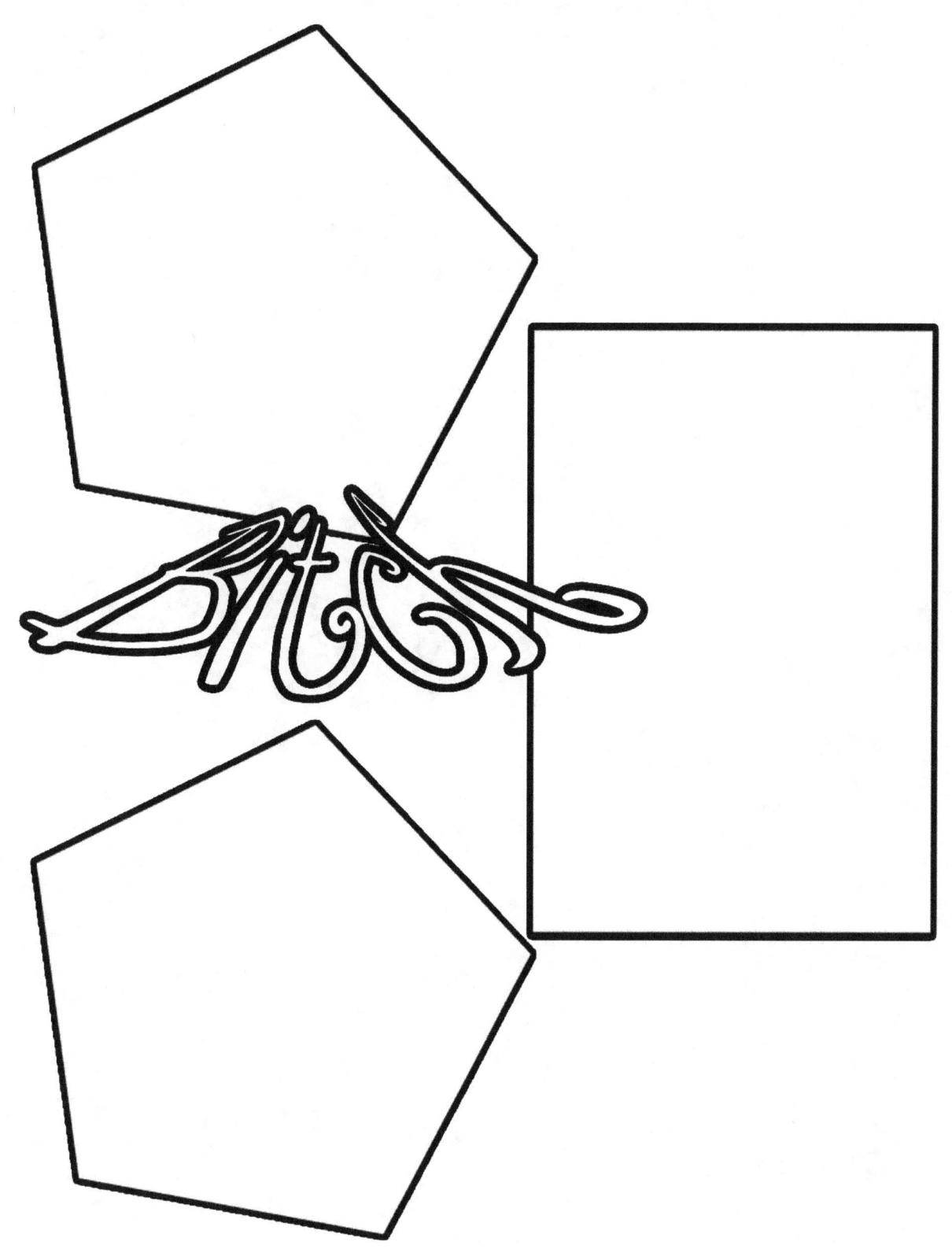

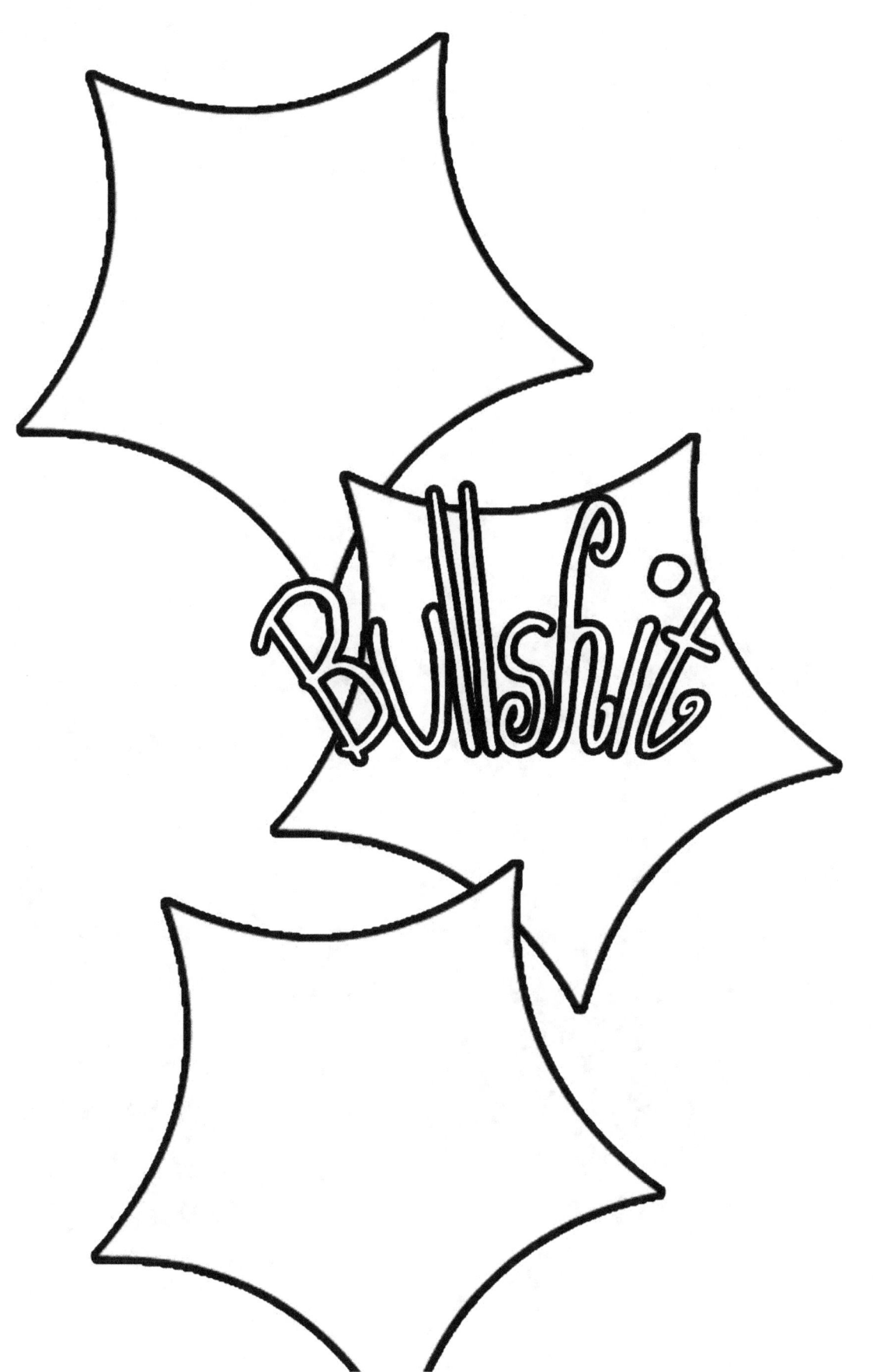

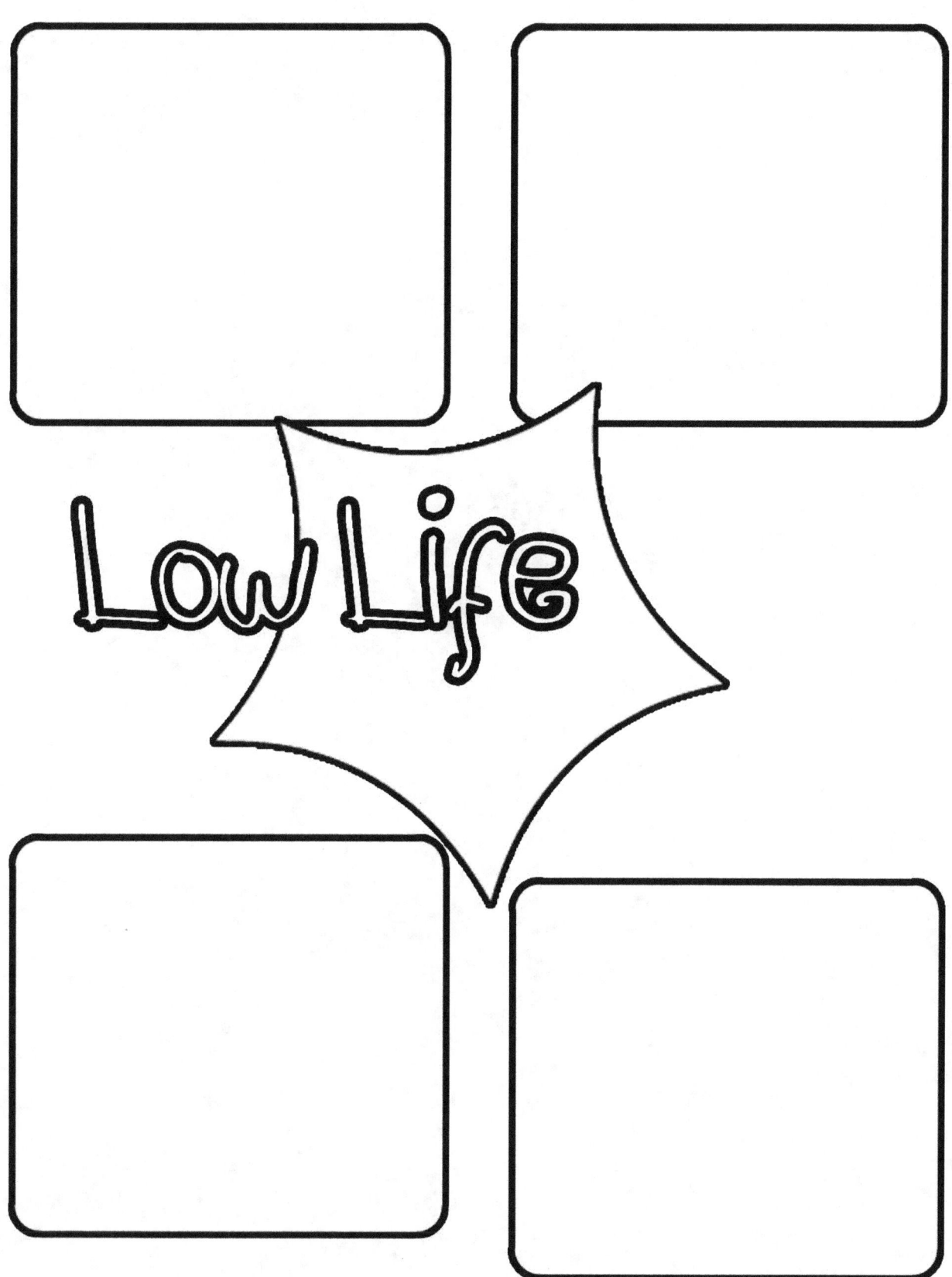

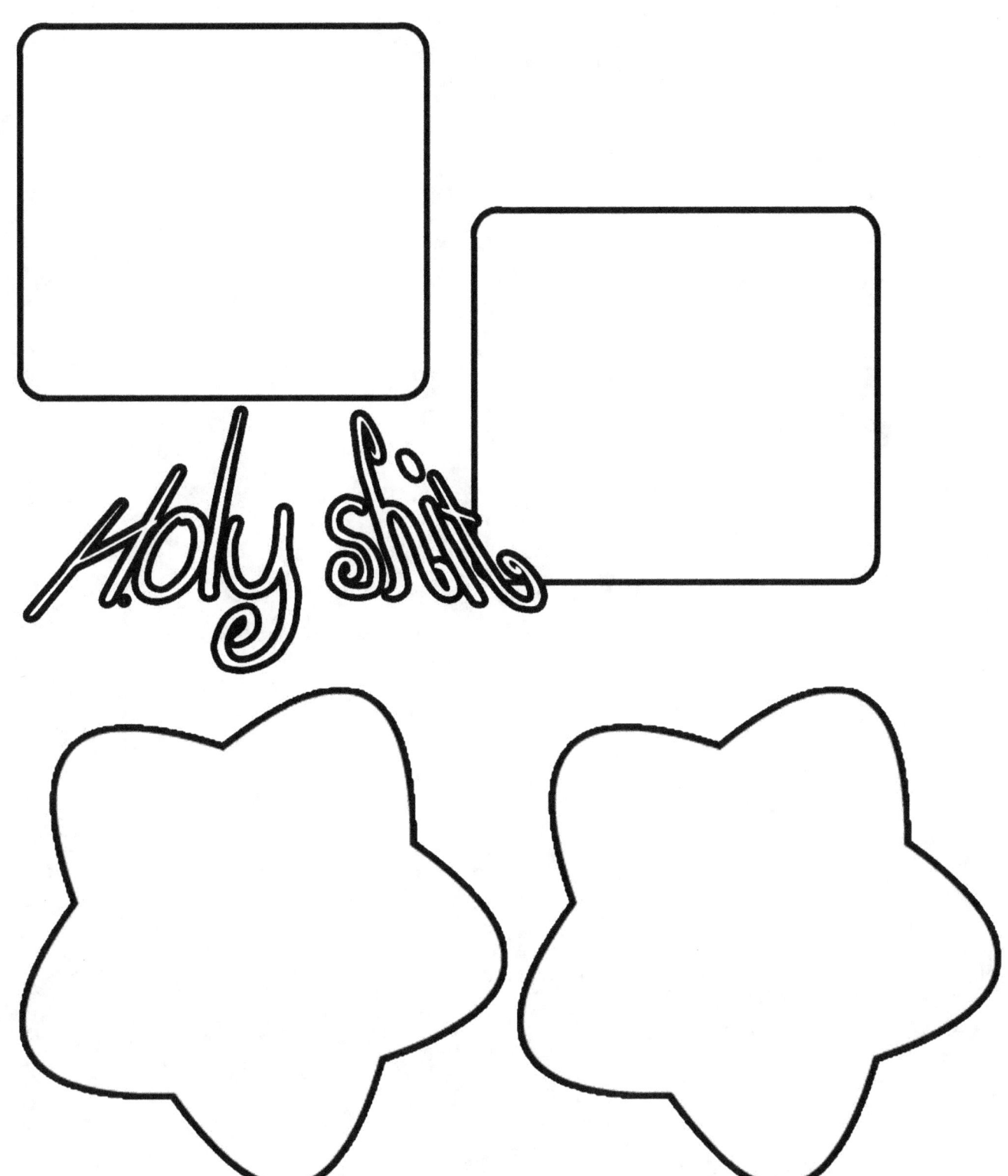

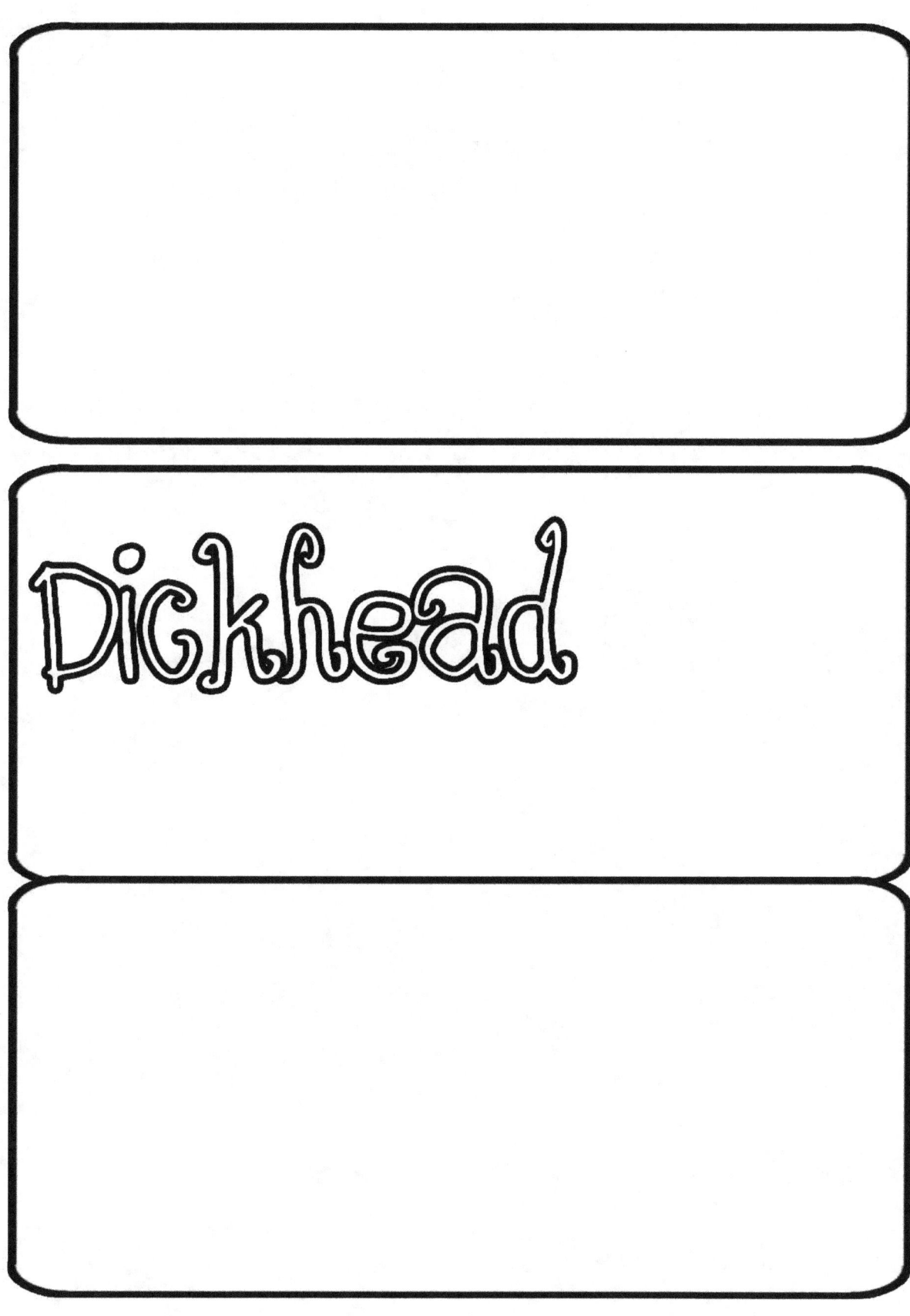

Dickhead

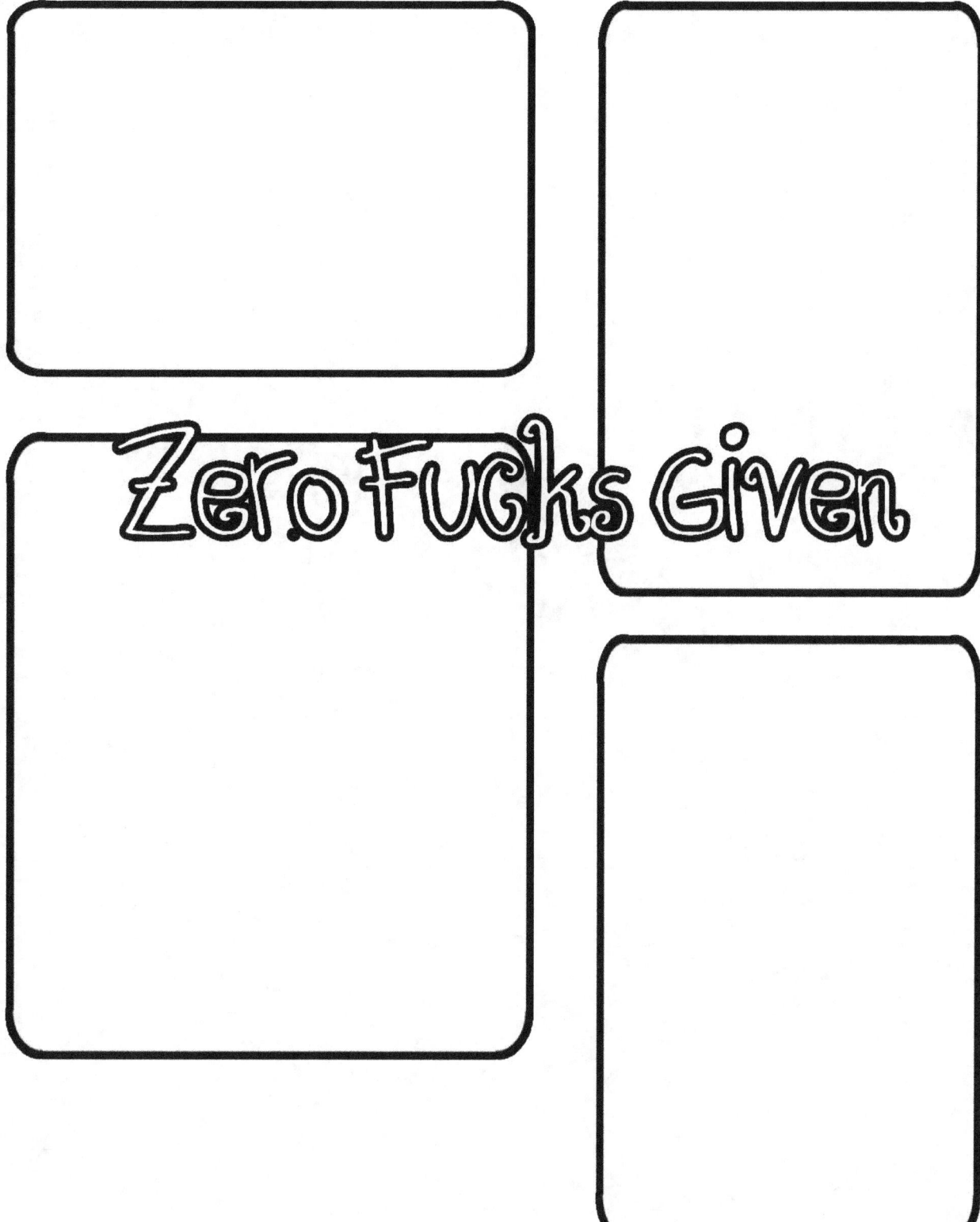

Zero Fucks Given

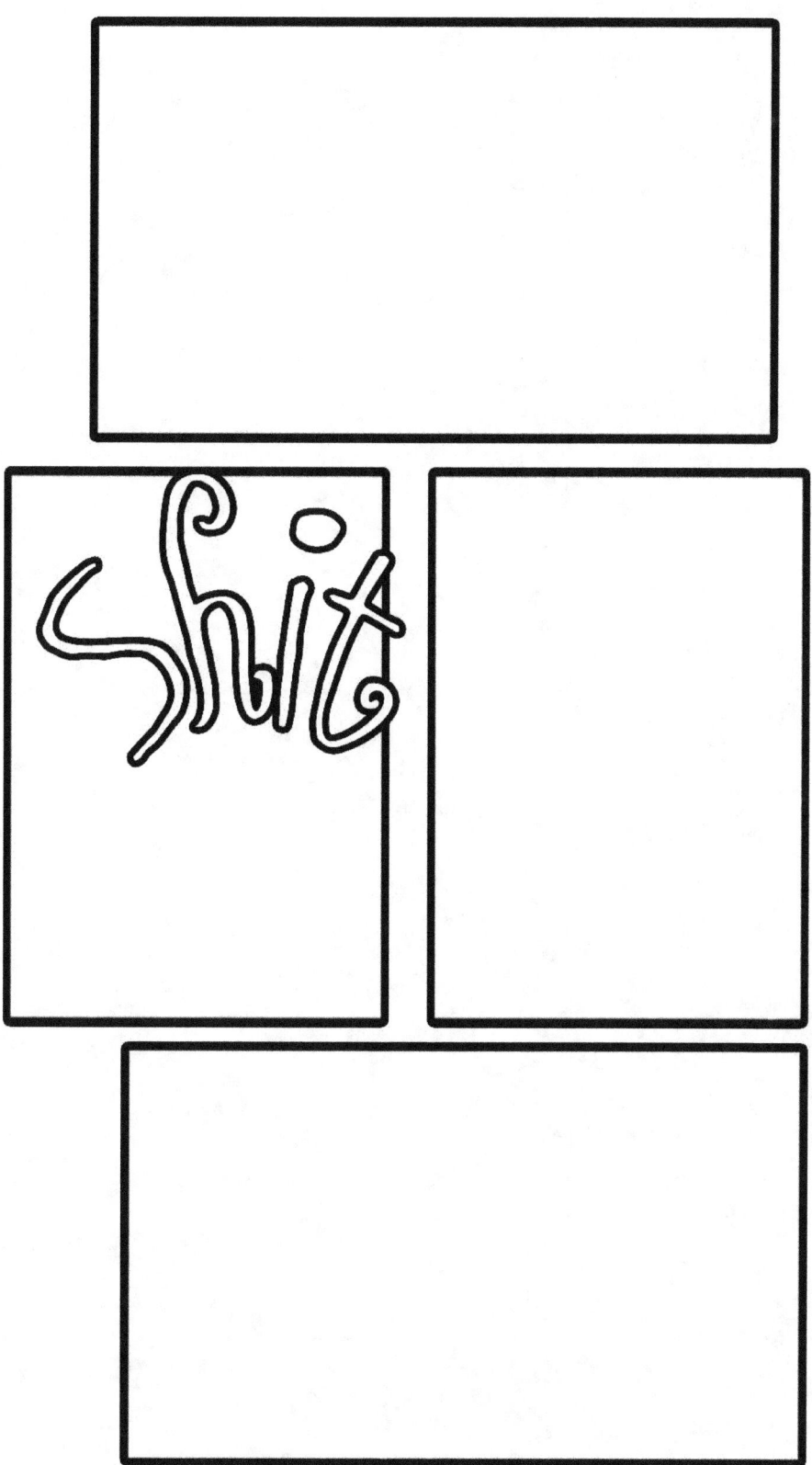

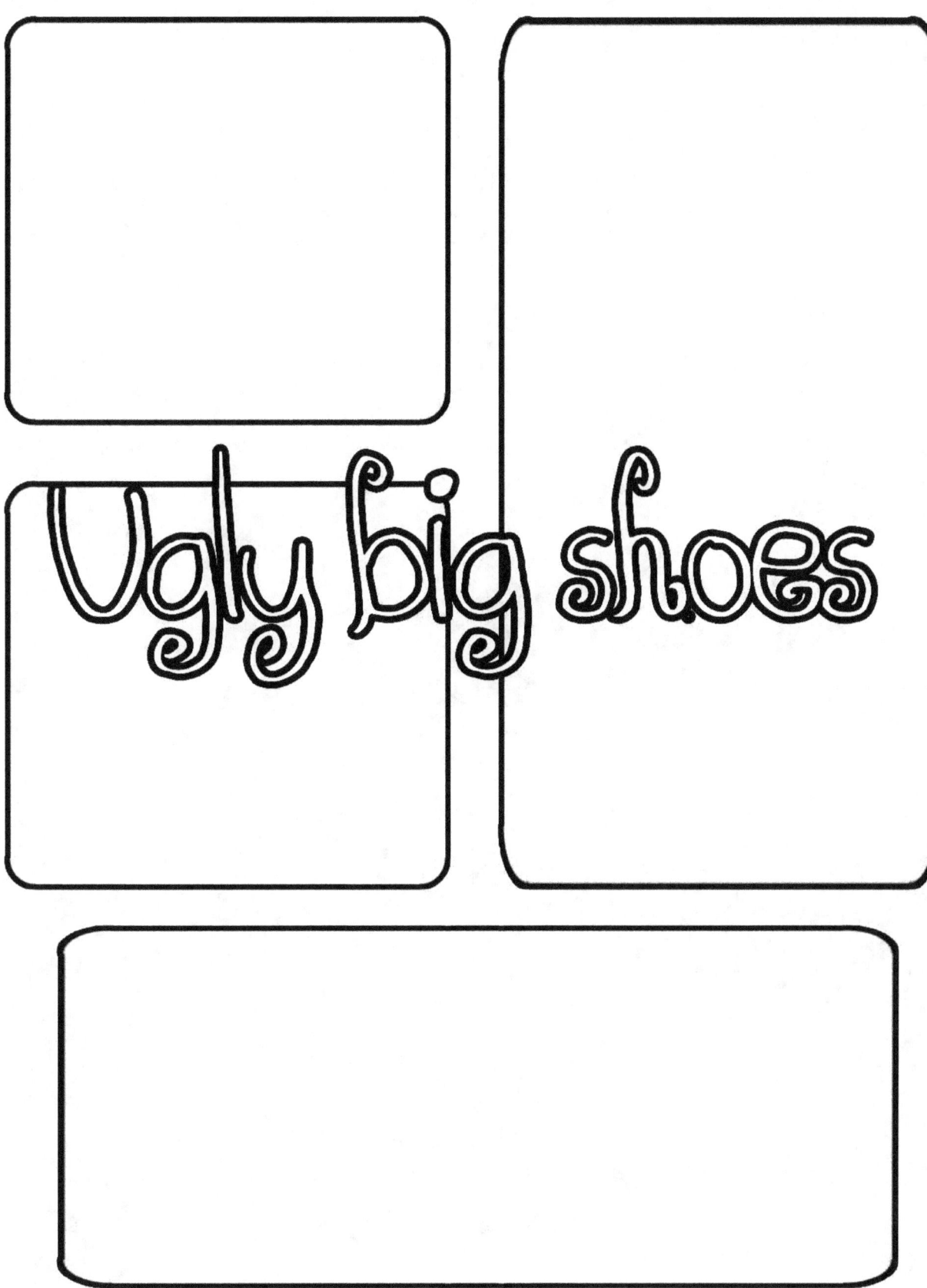

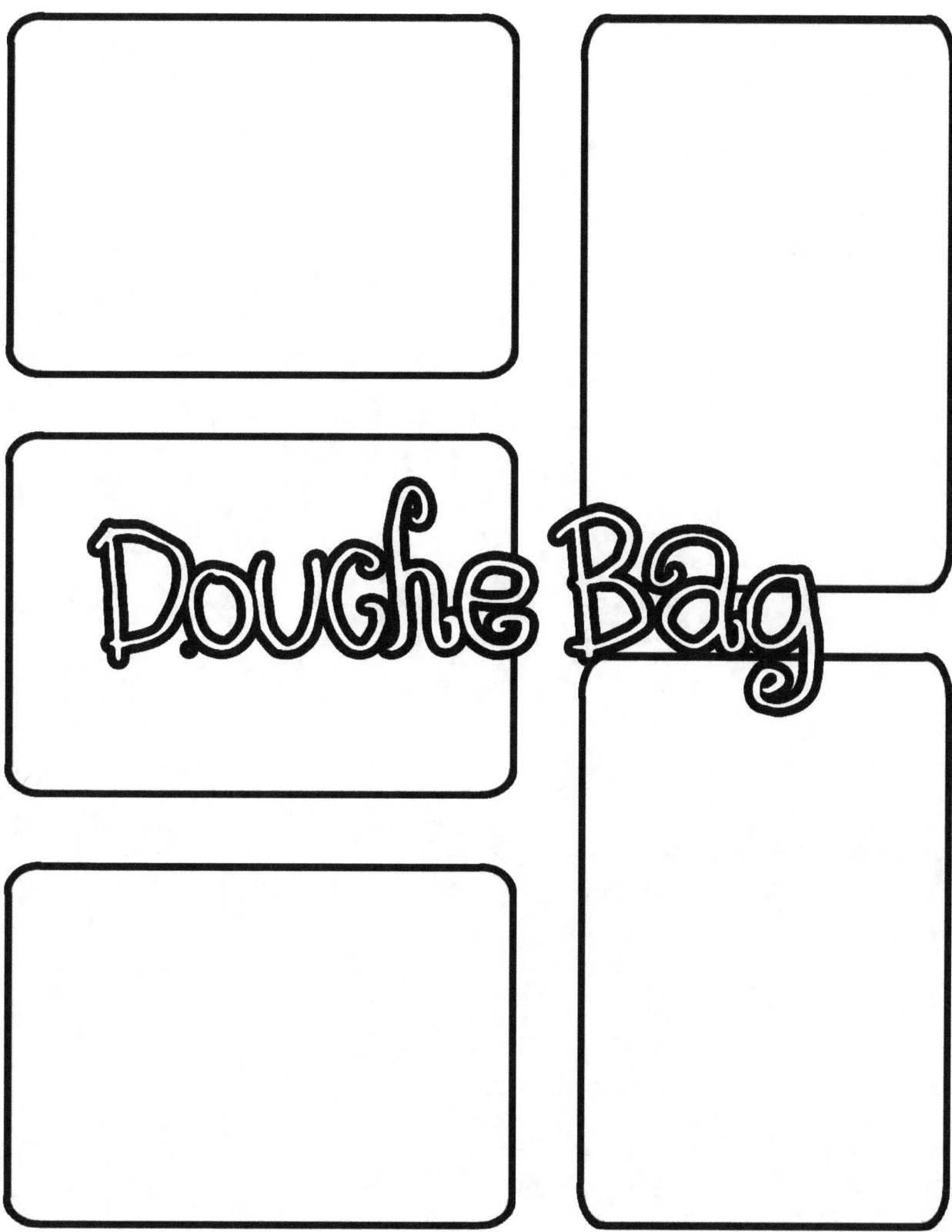

Douche Bag

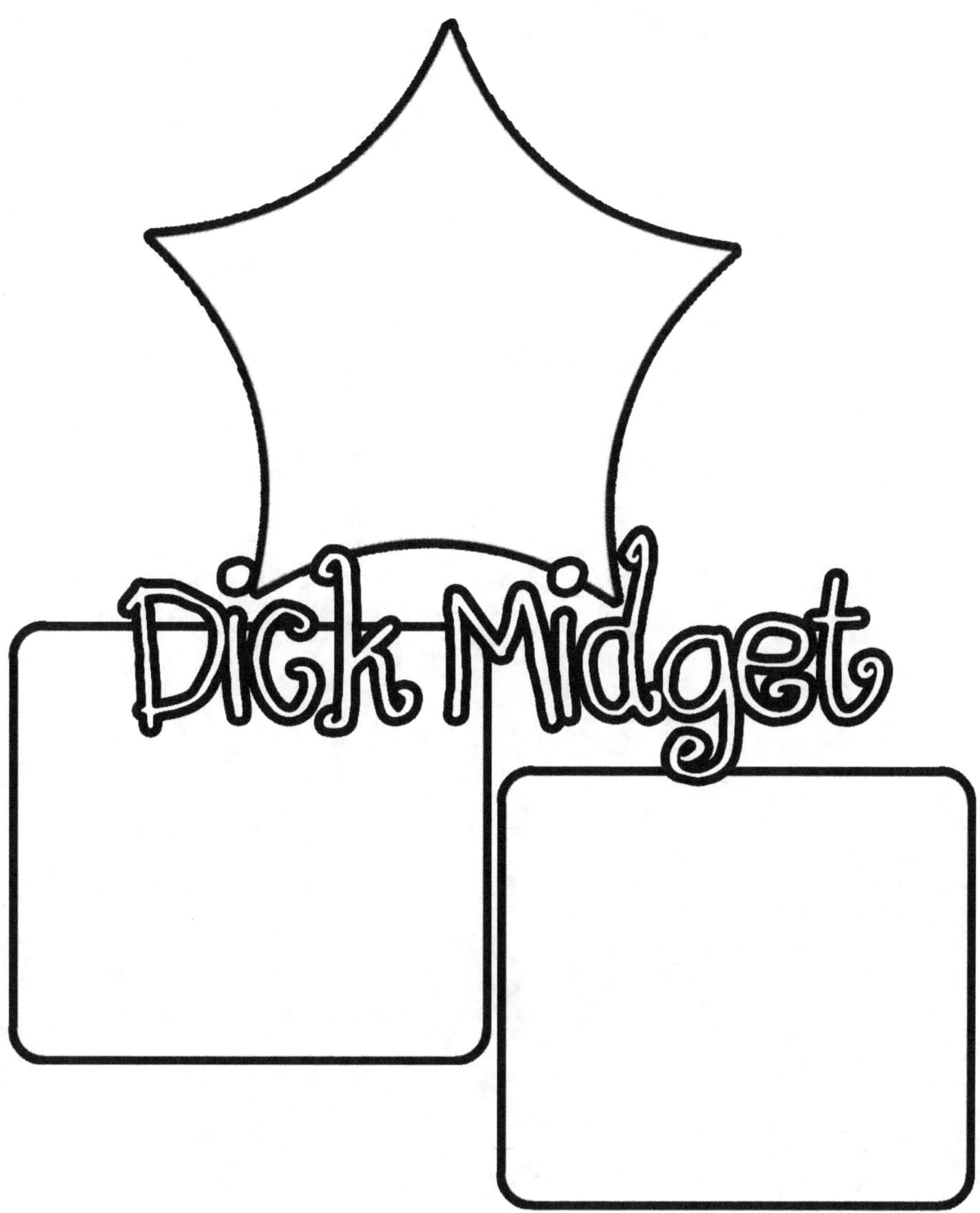

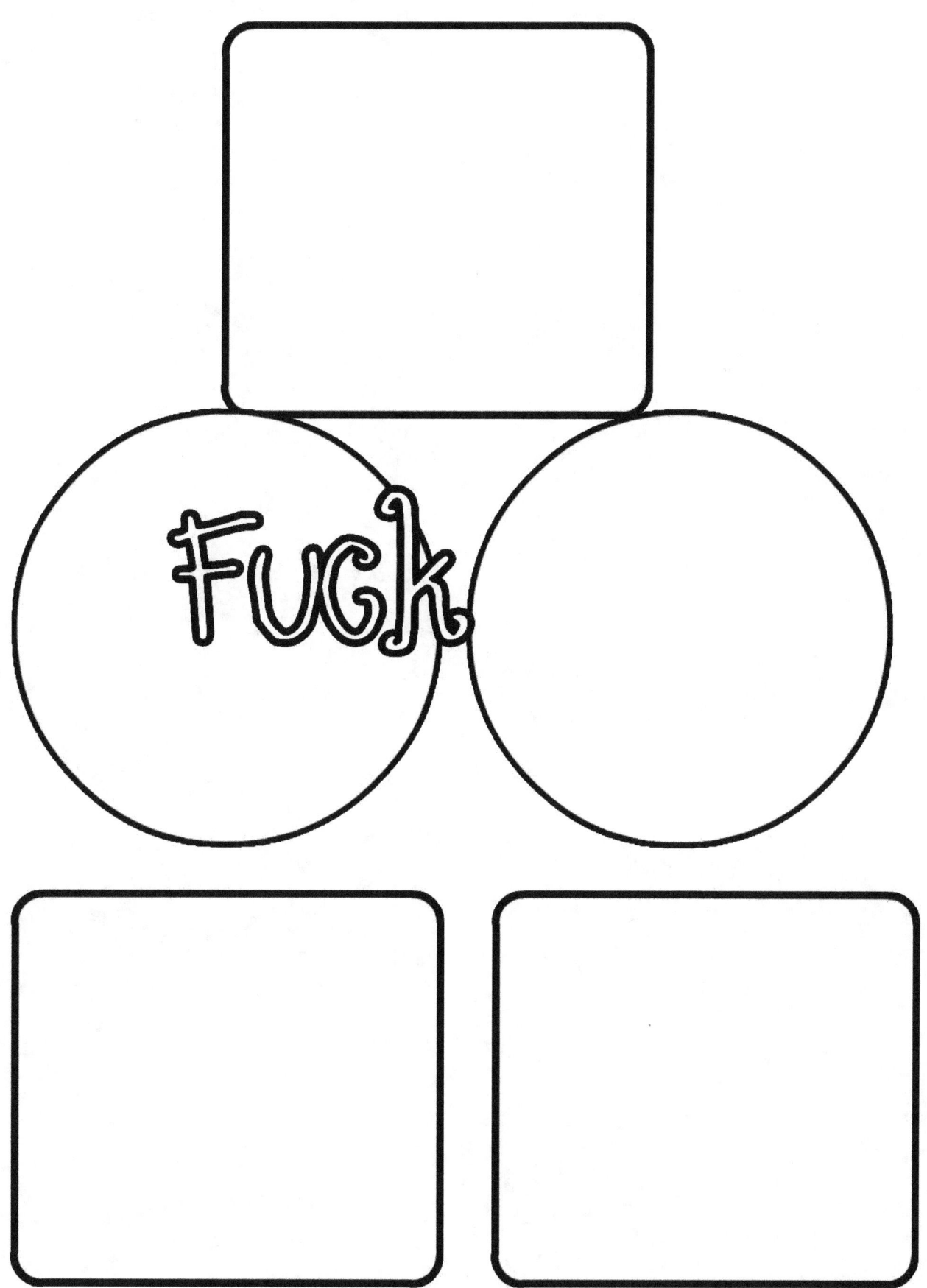

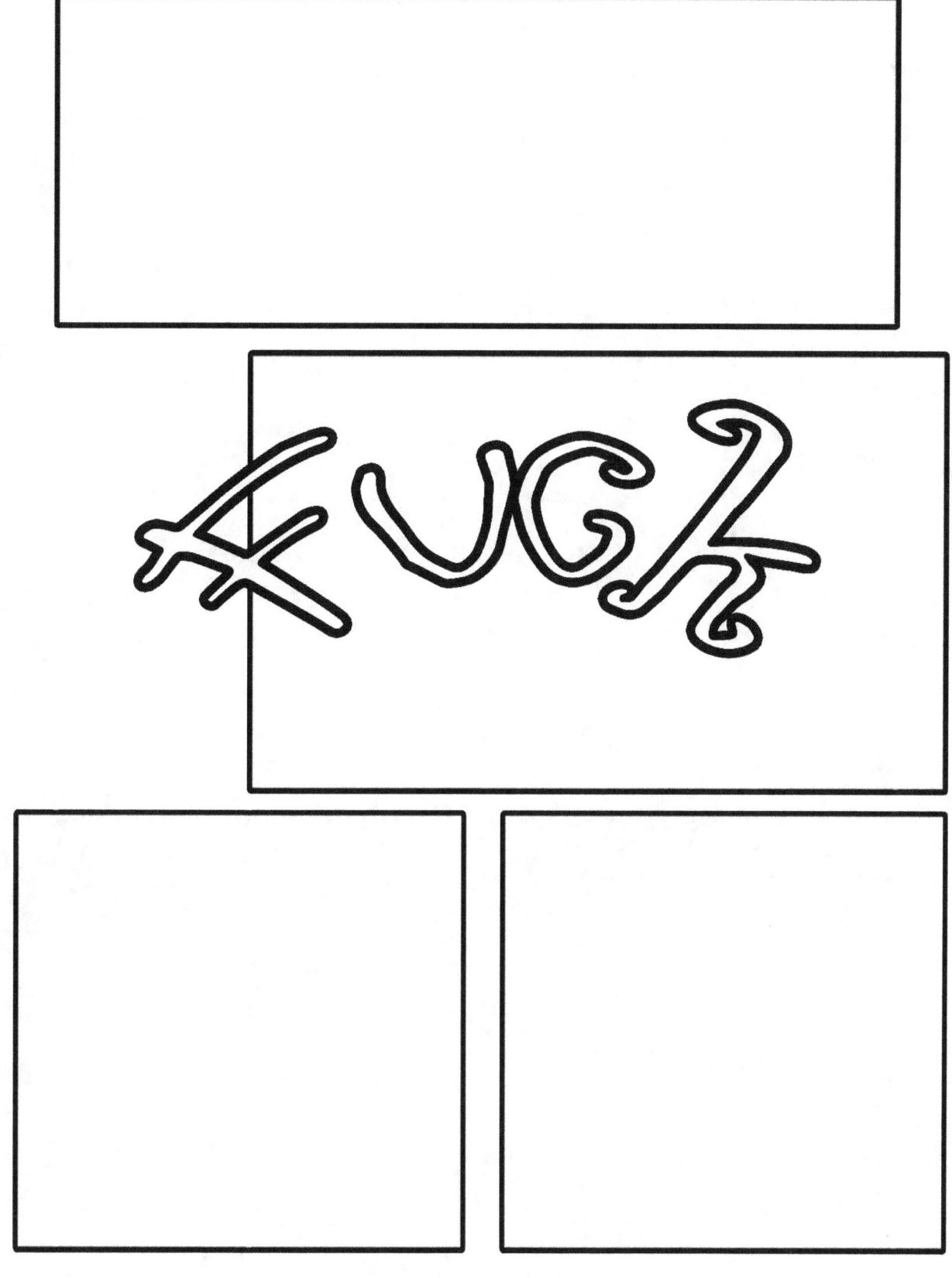

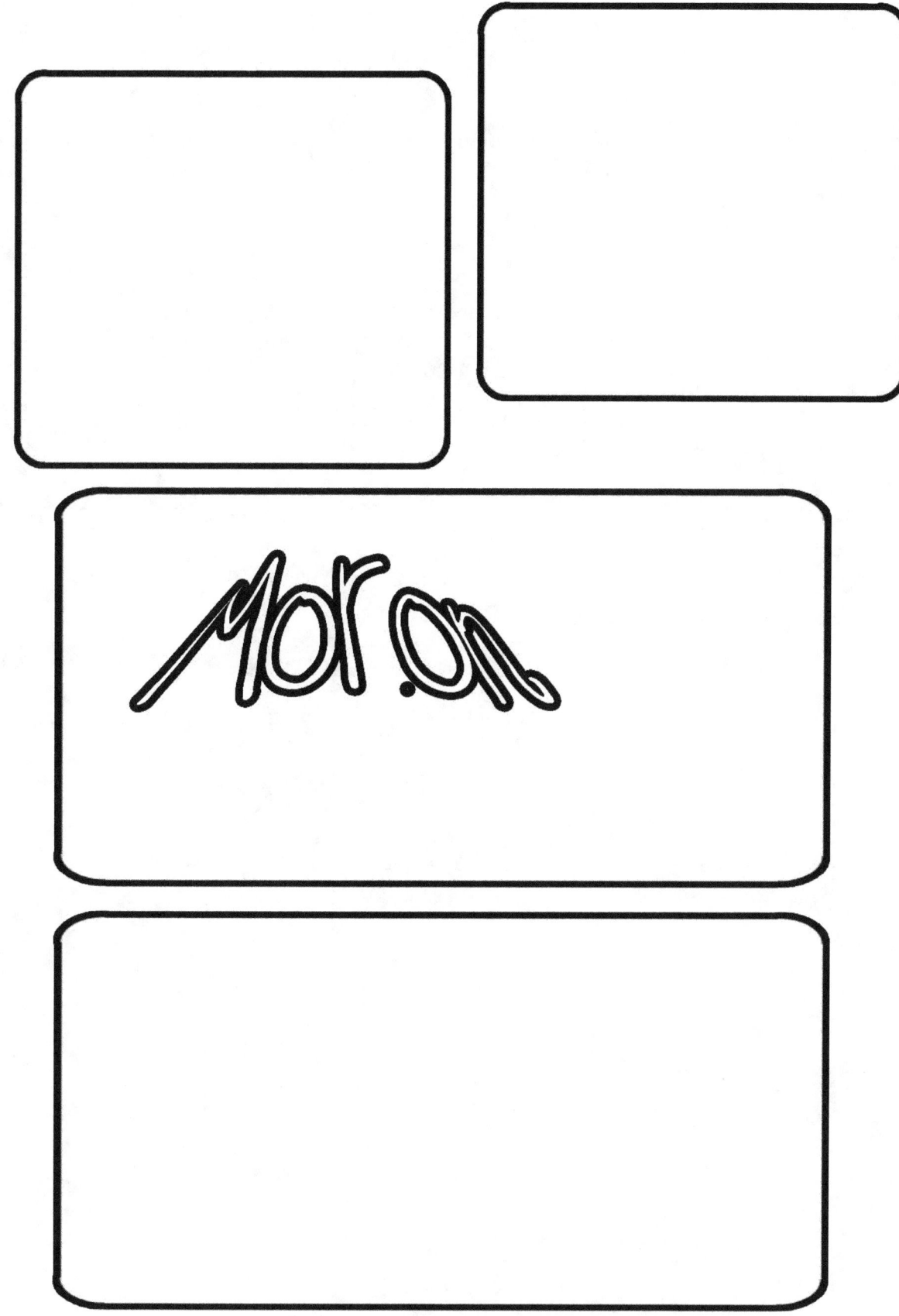

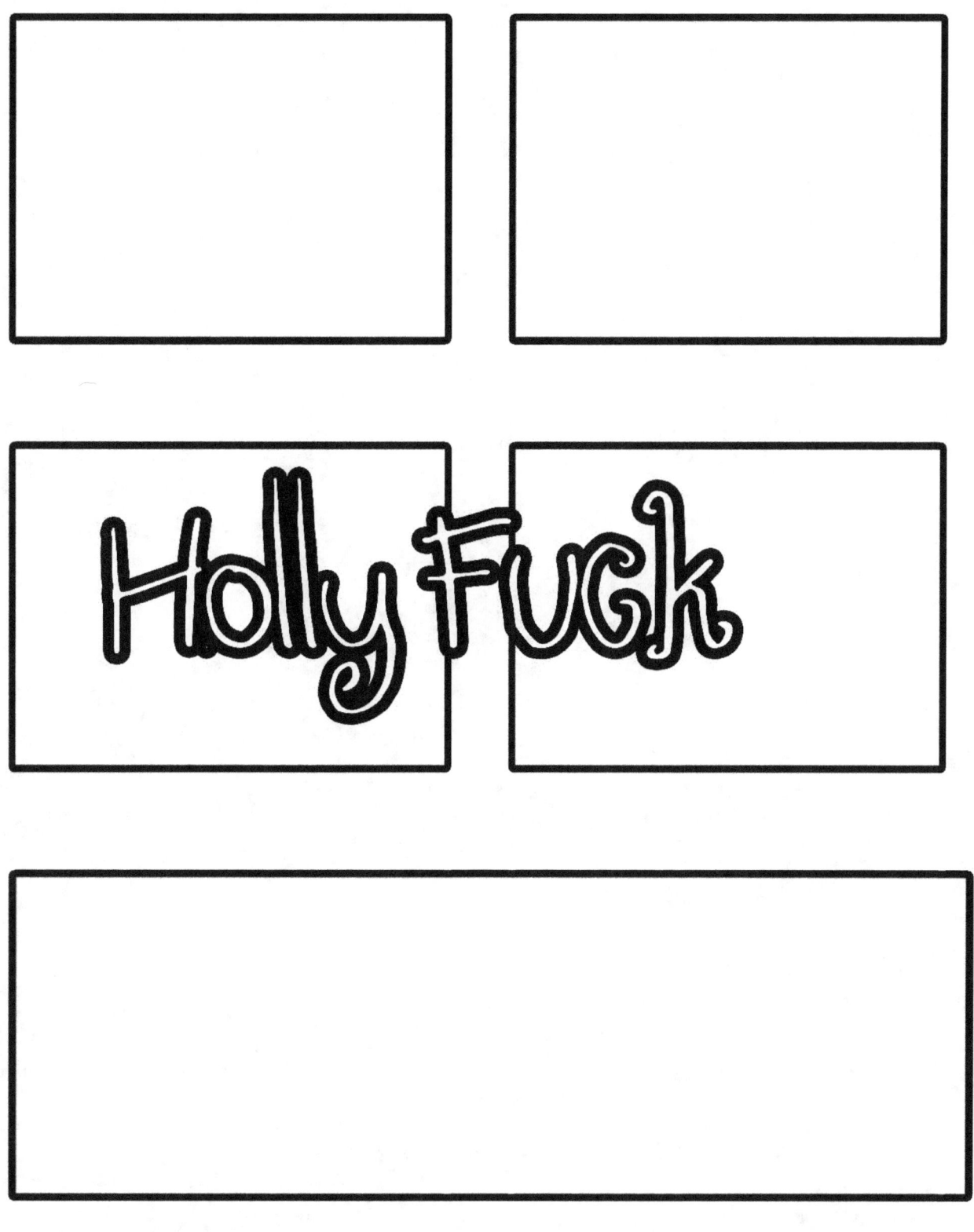

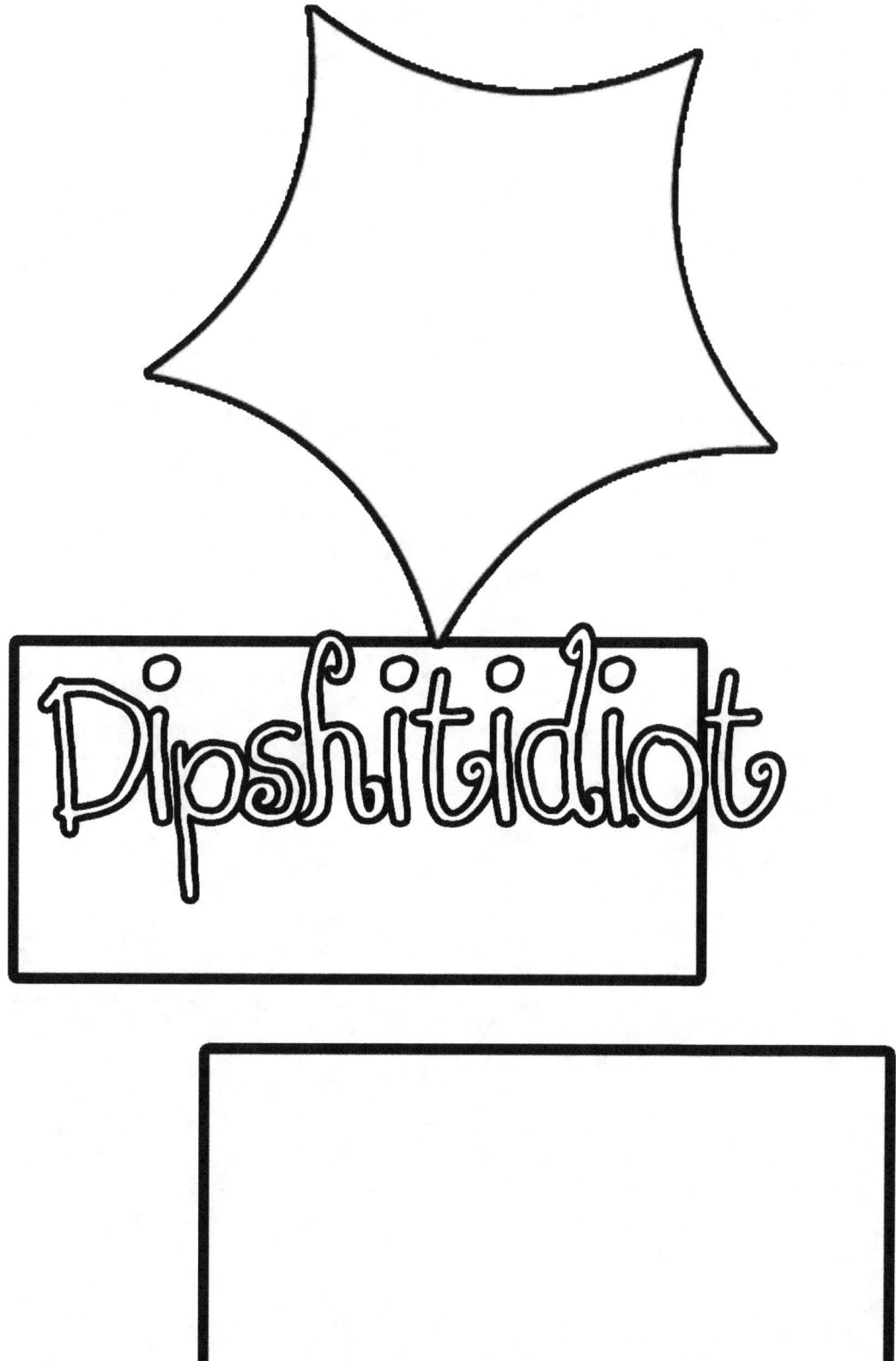

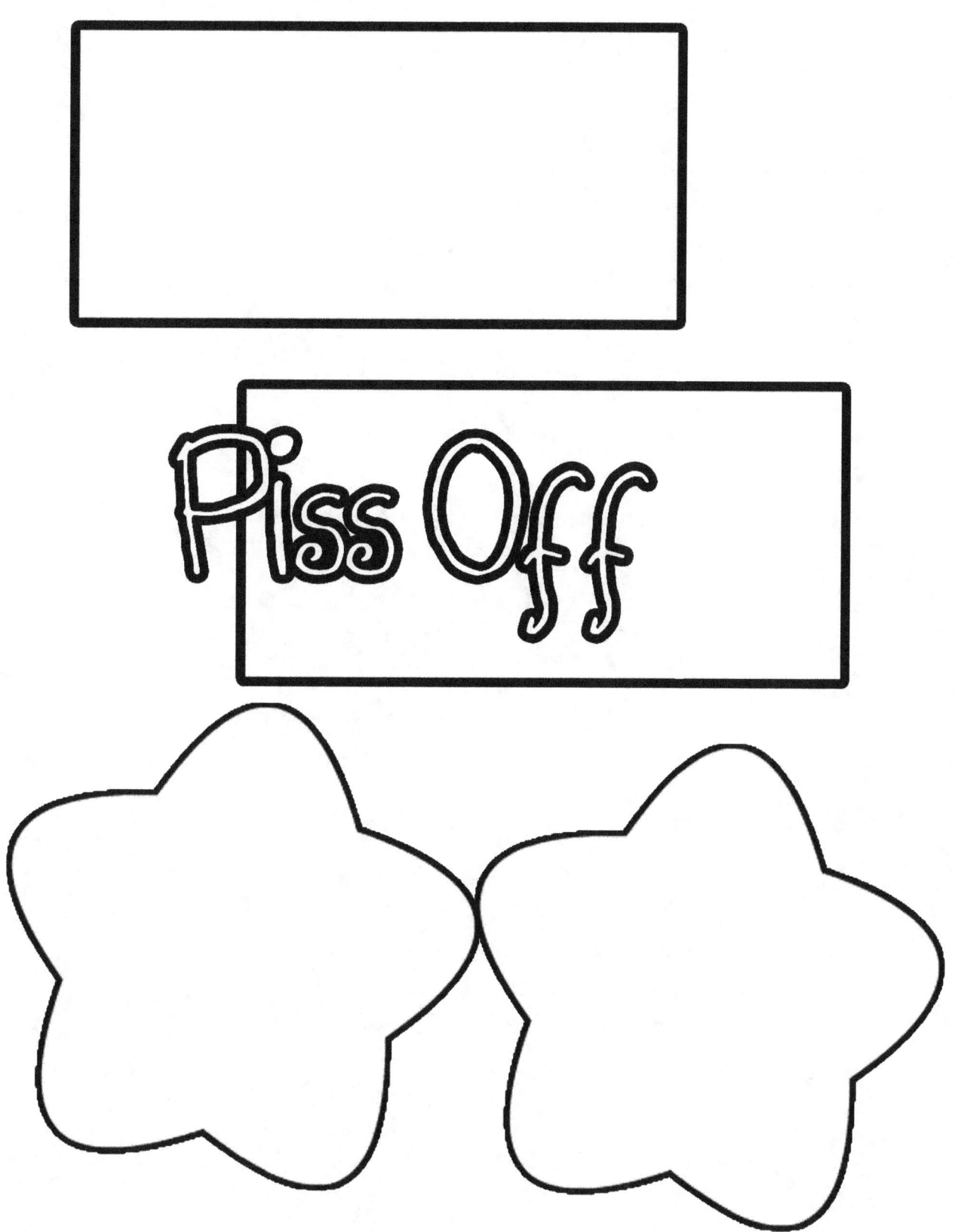

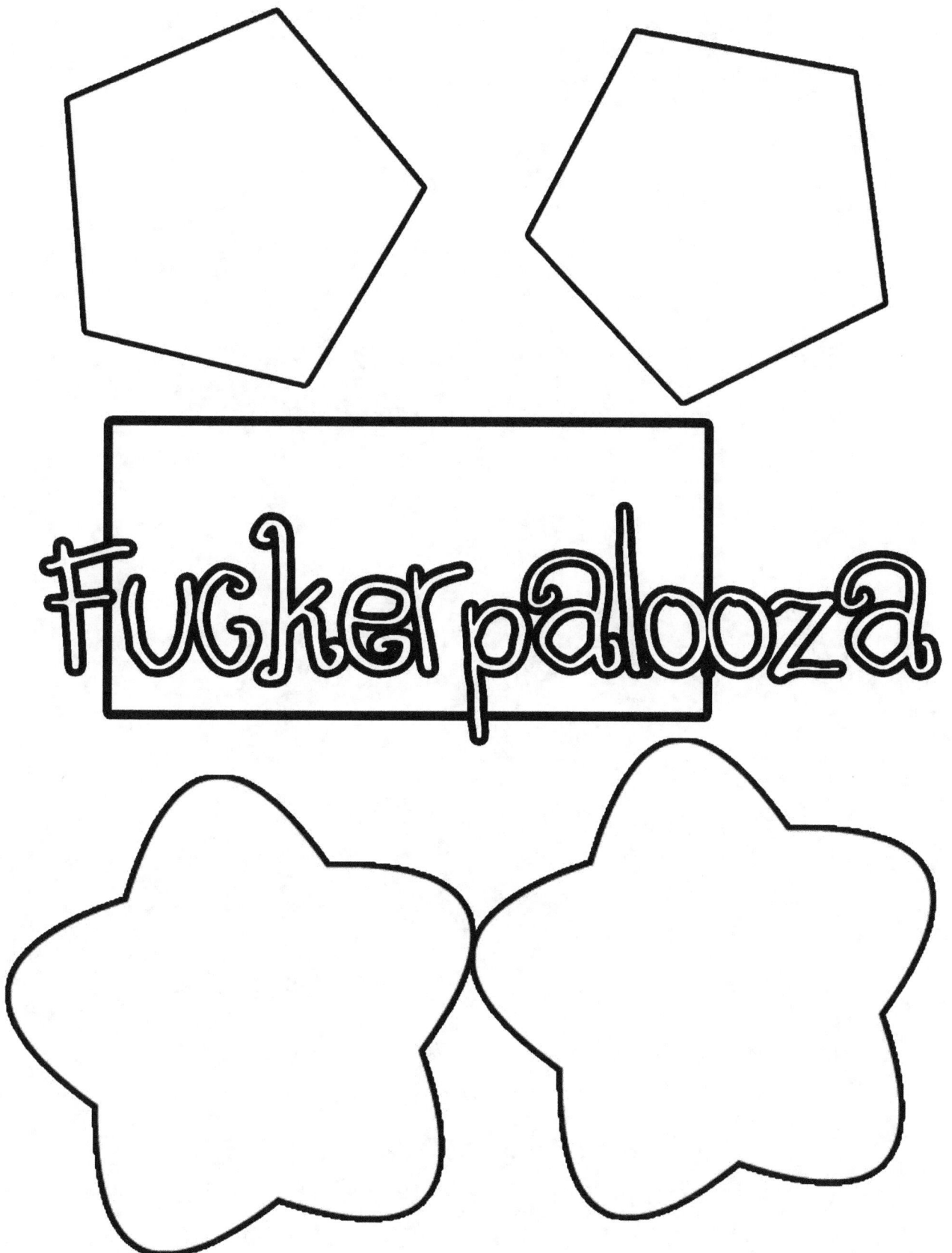

Fuck this Shit

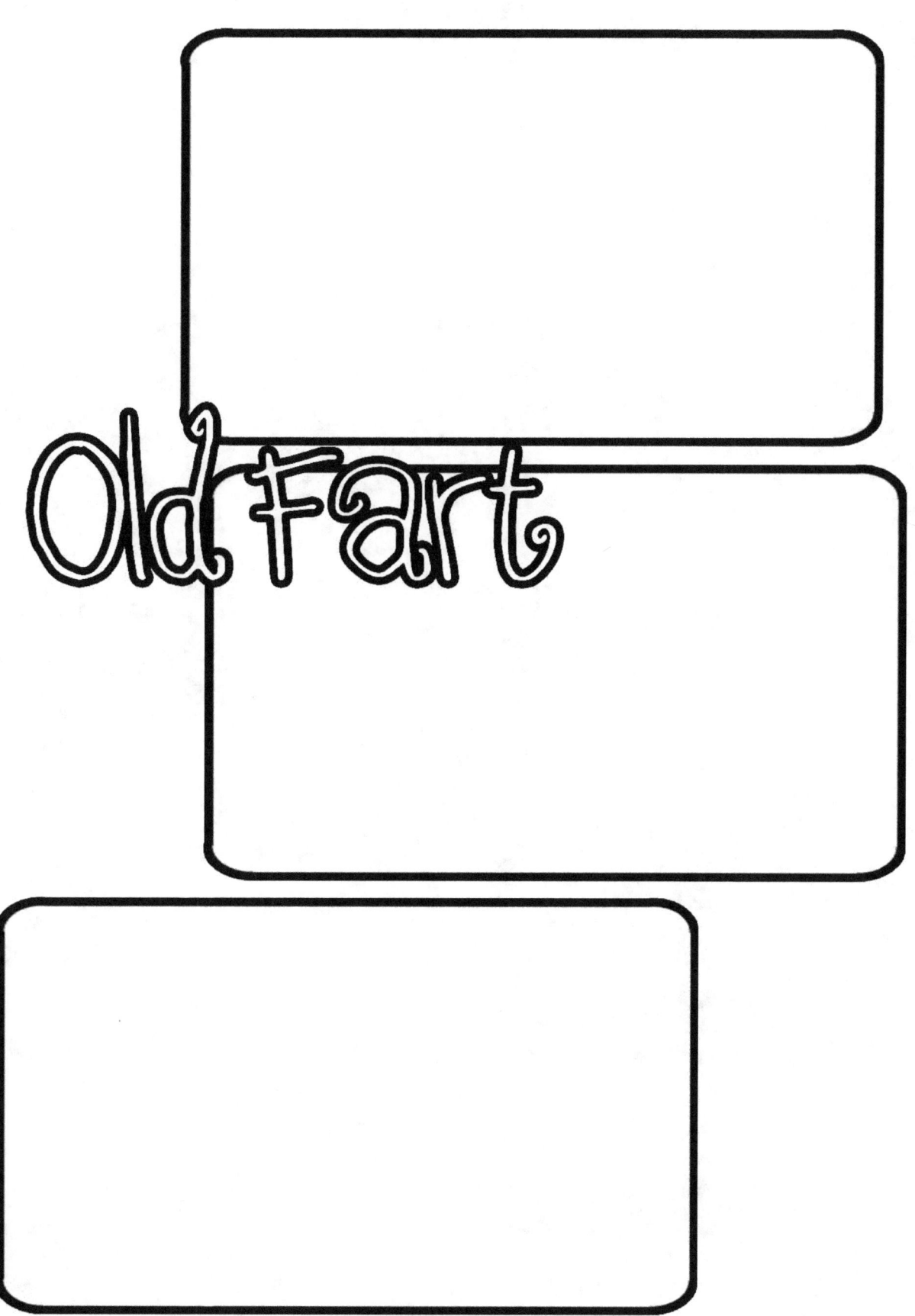

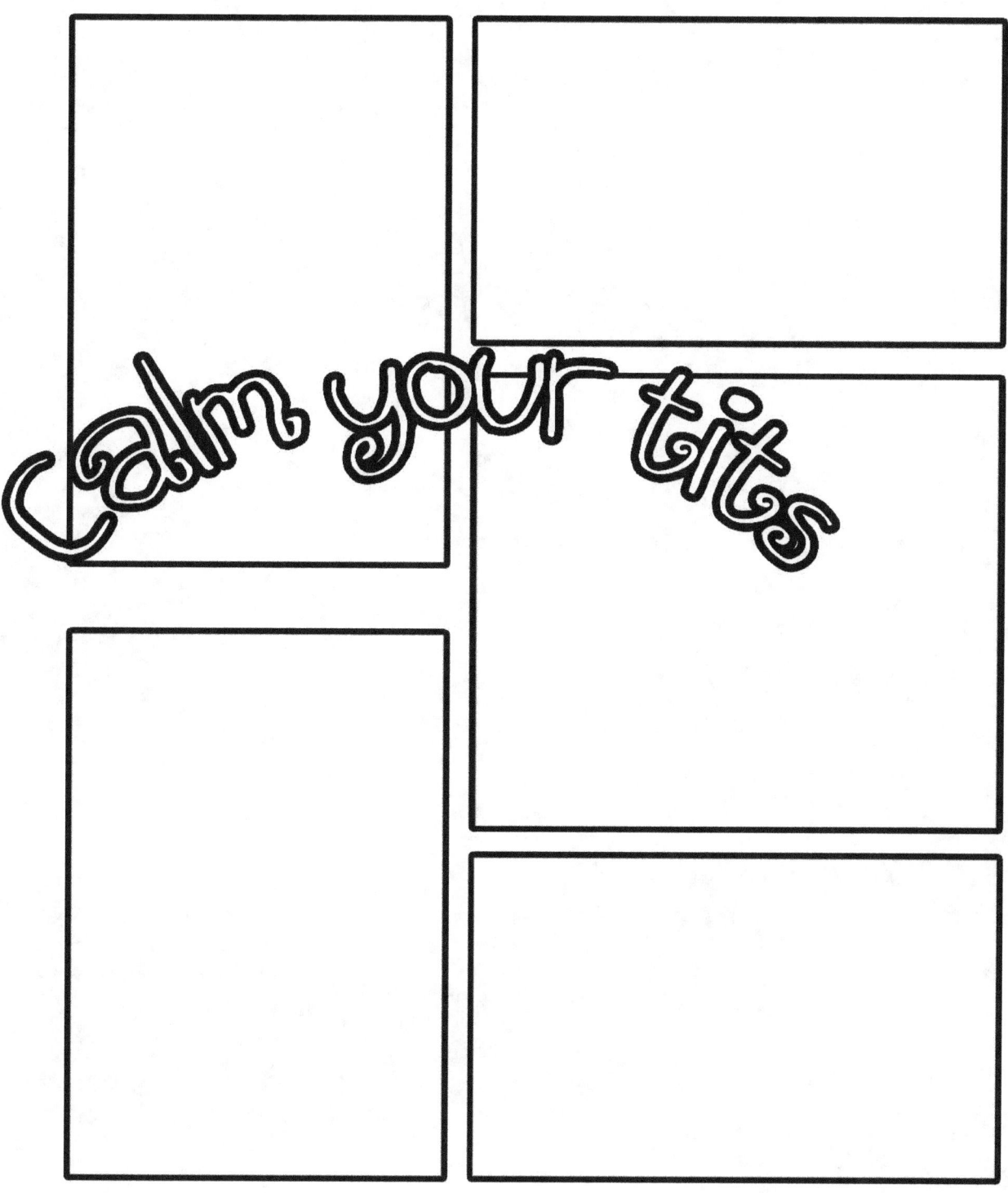

Motherfucker

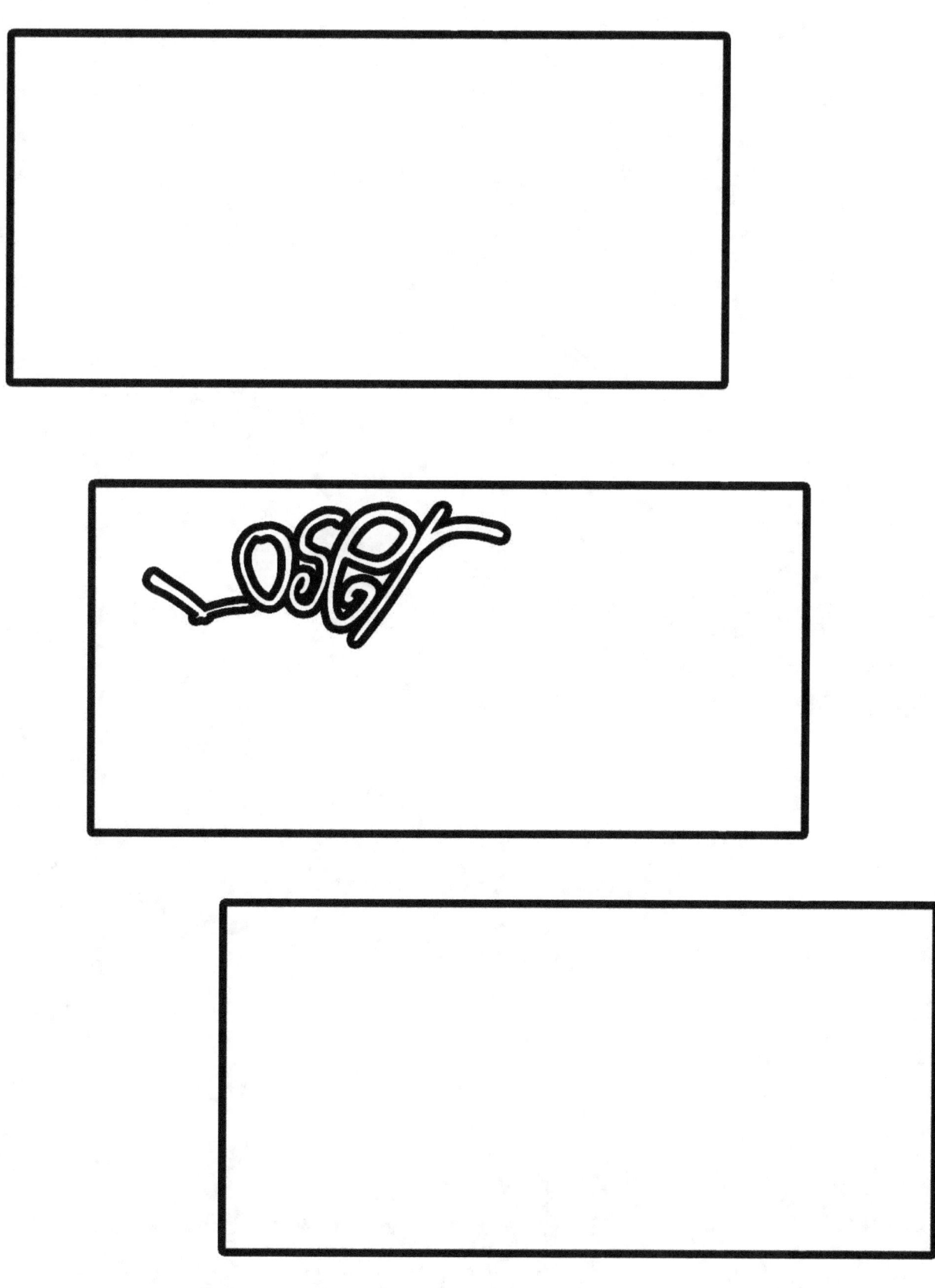

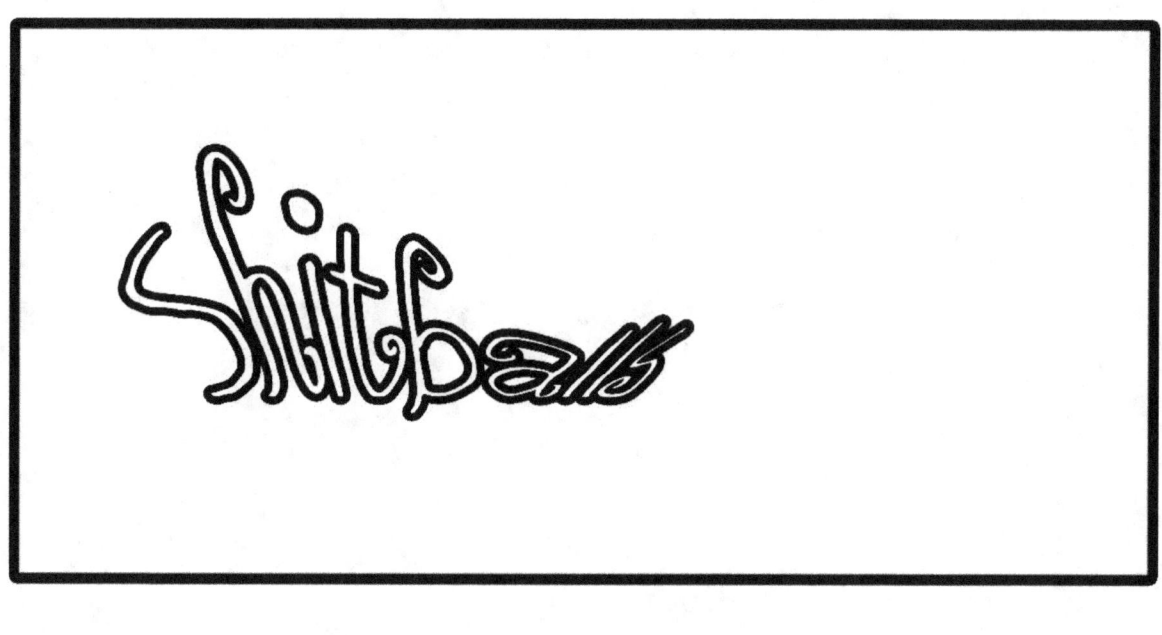

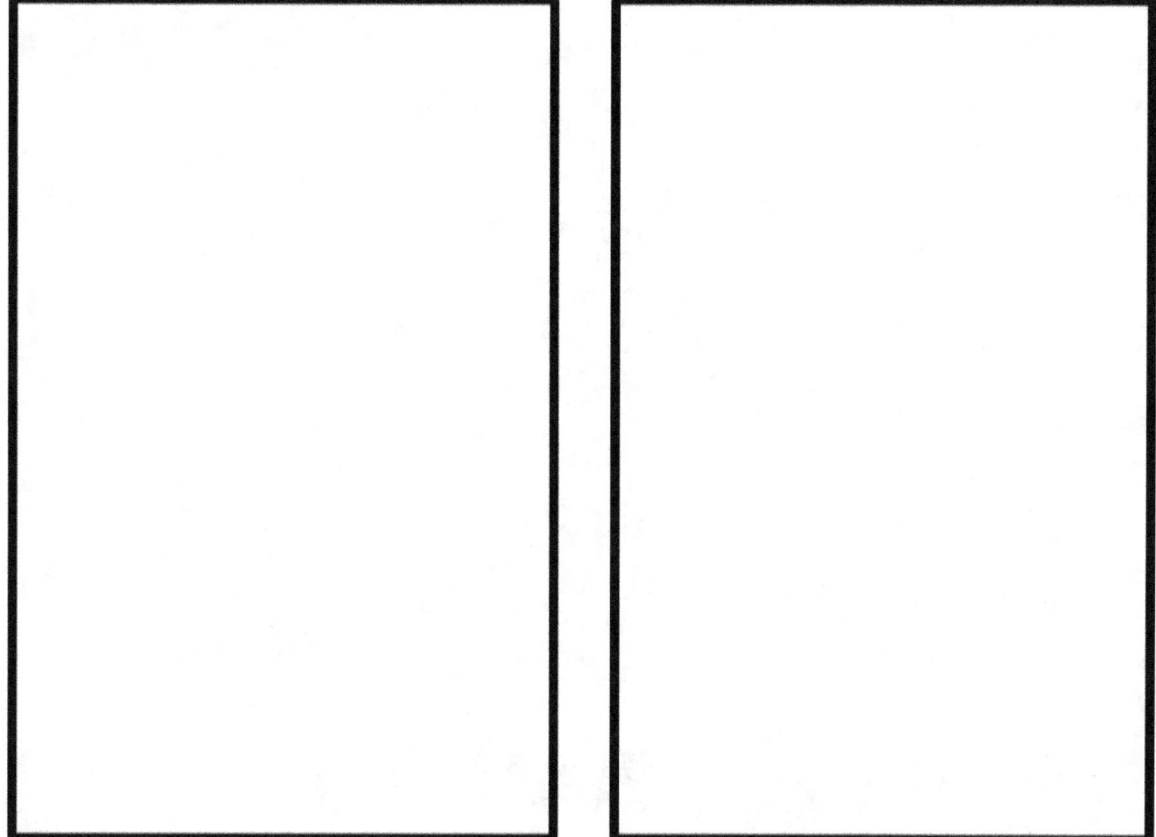

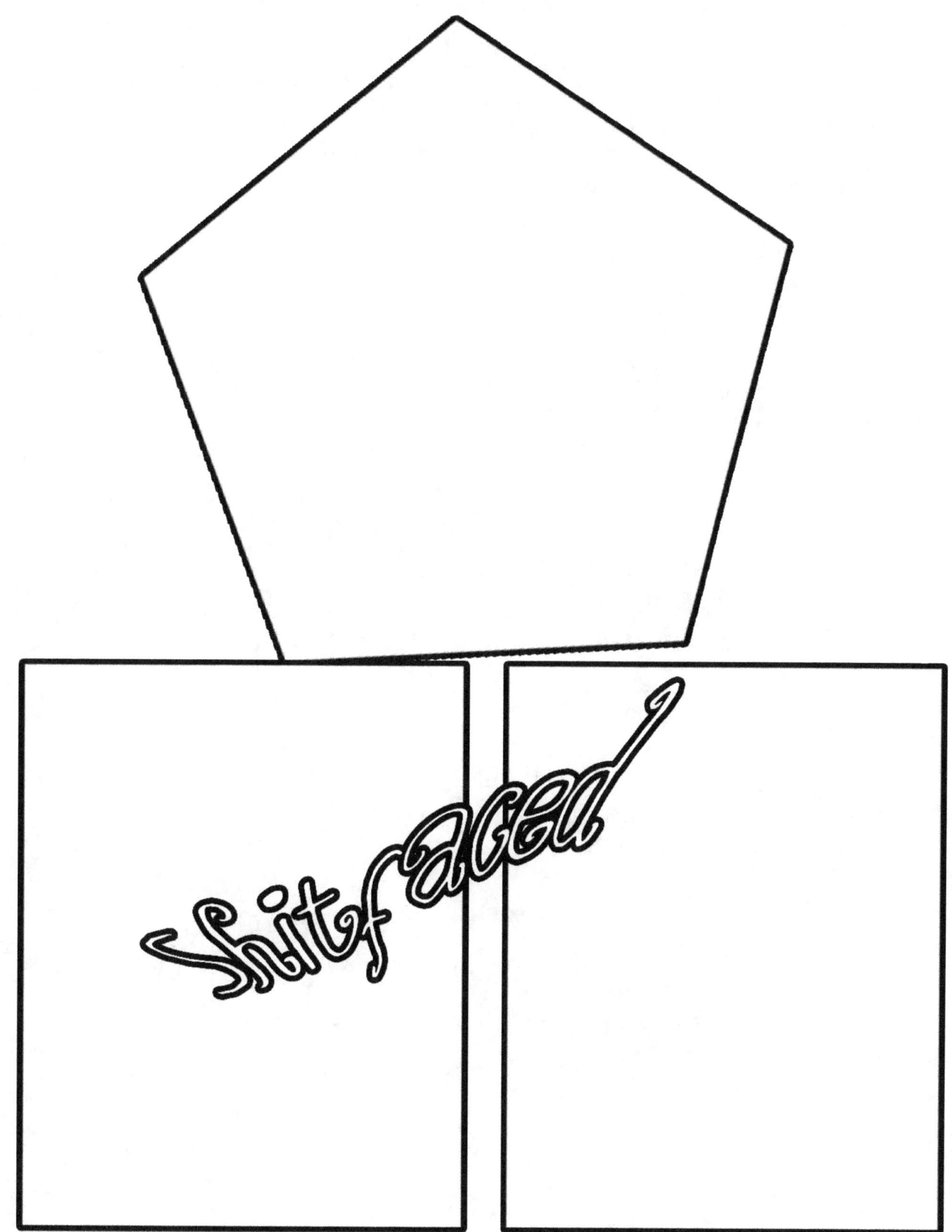

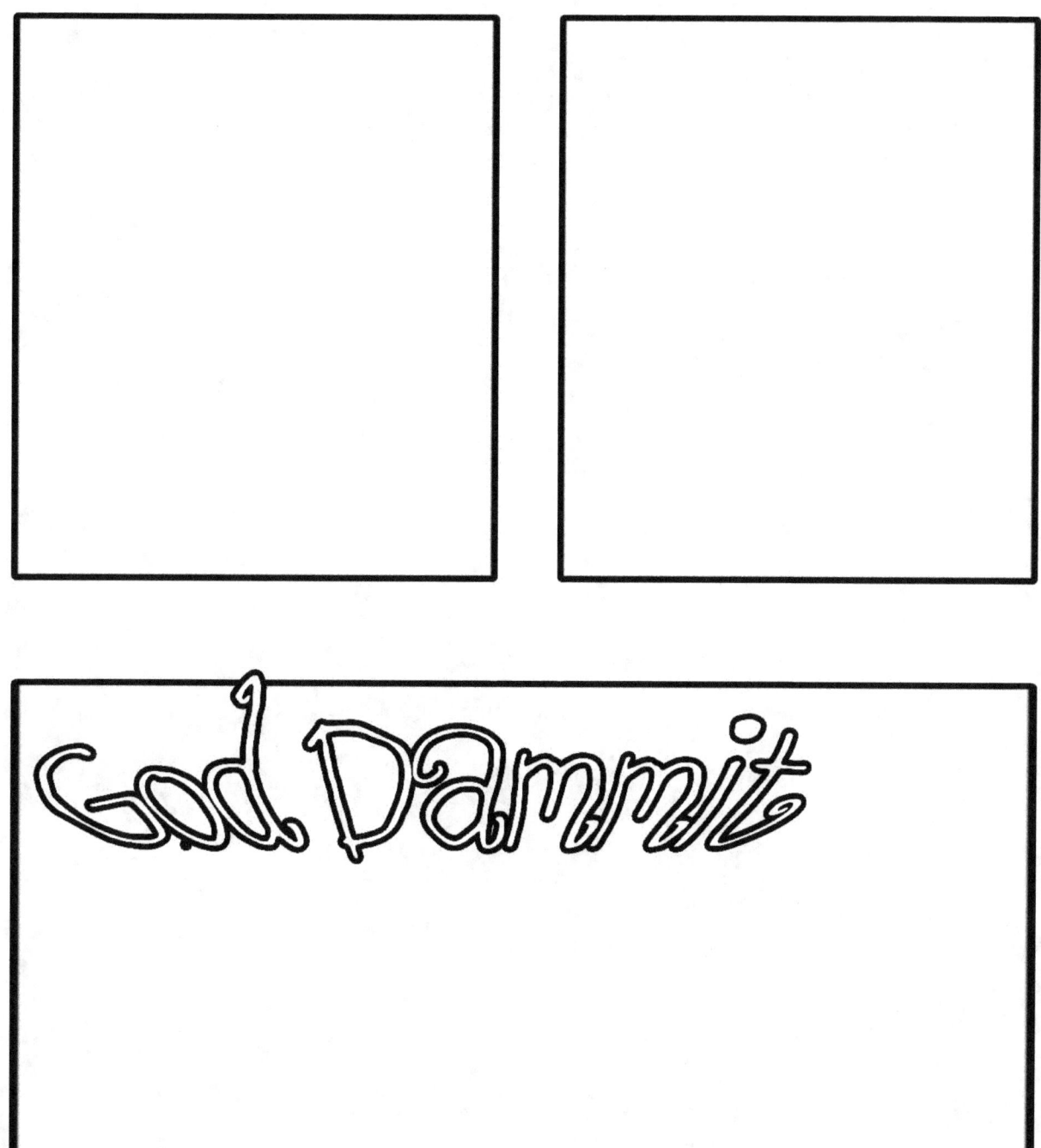

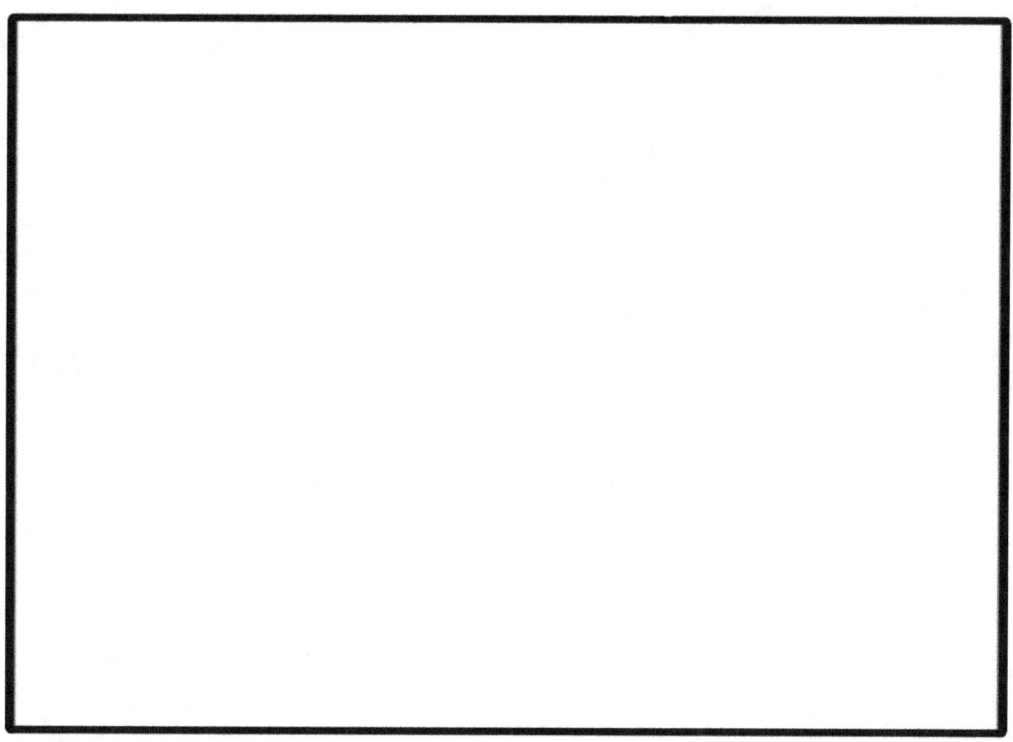

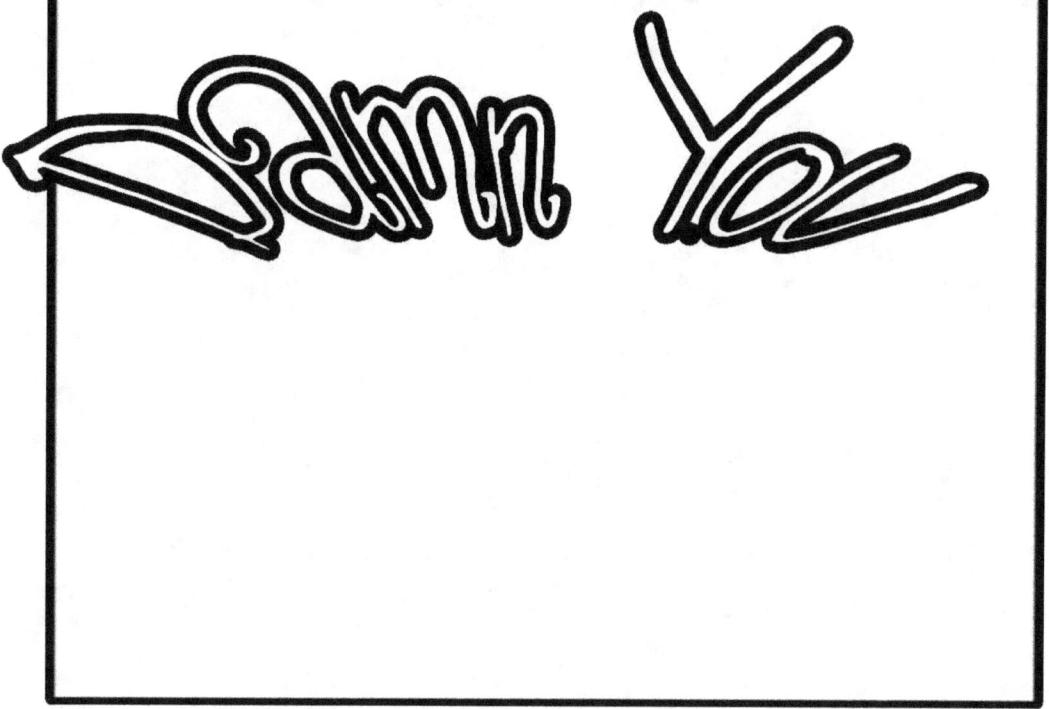

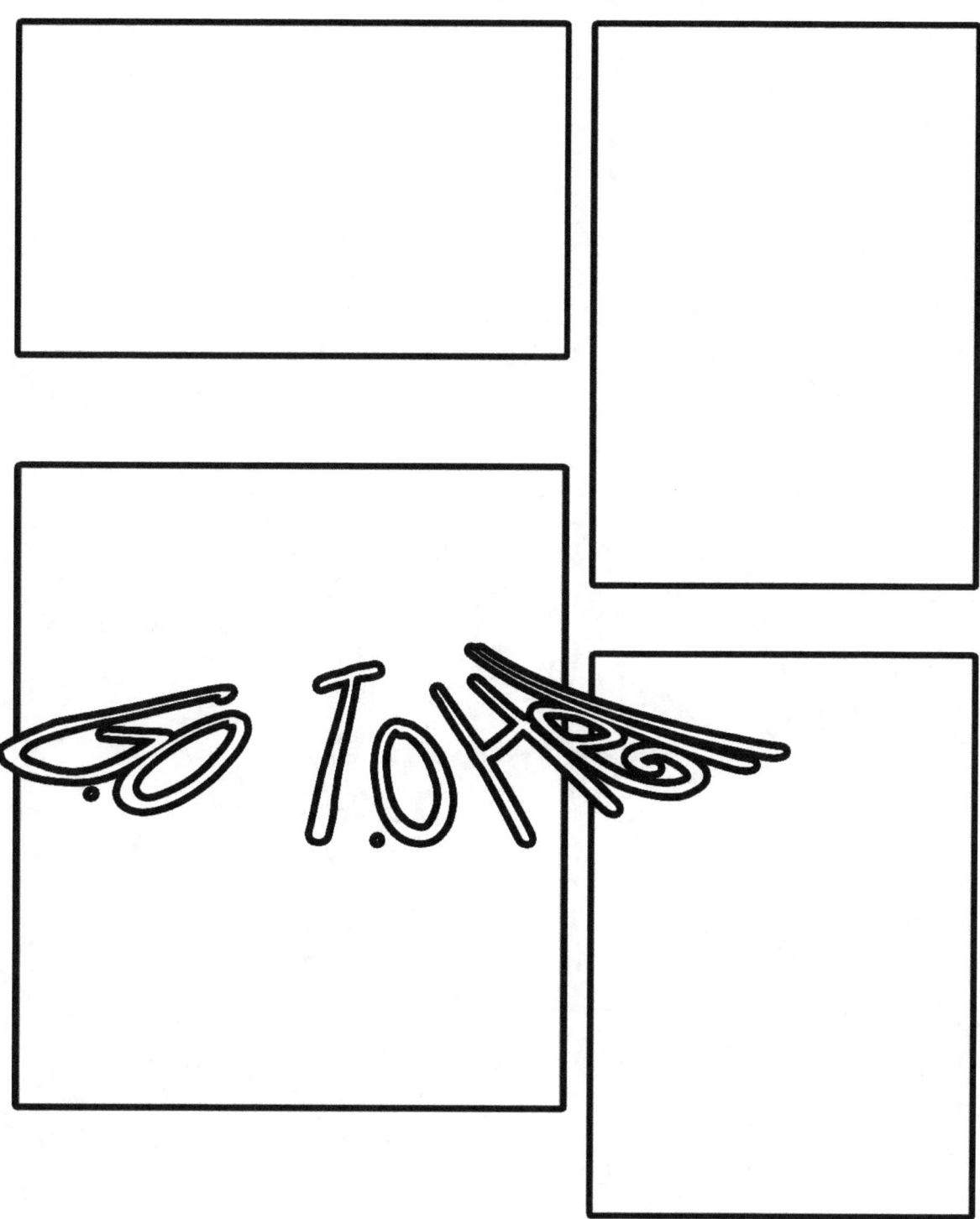

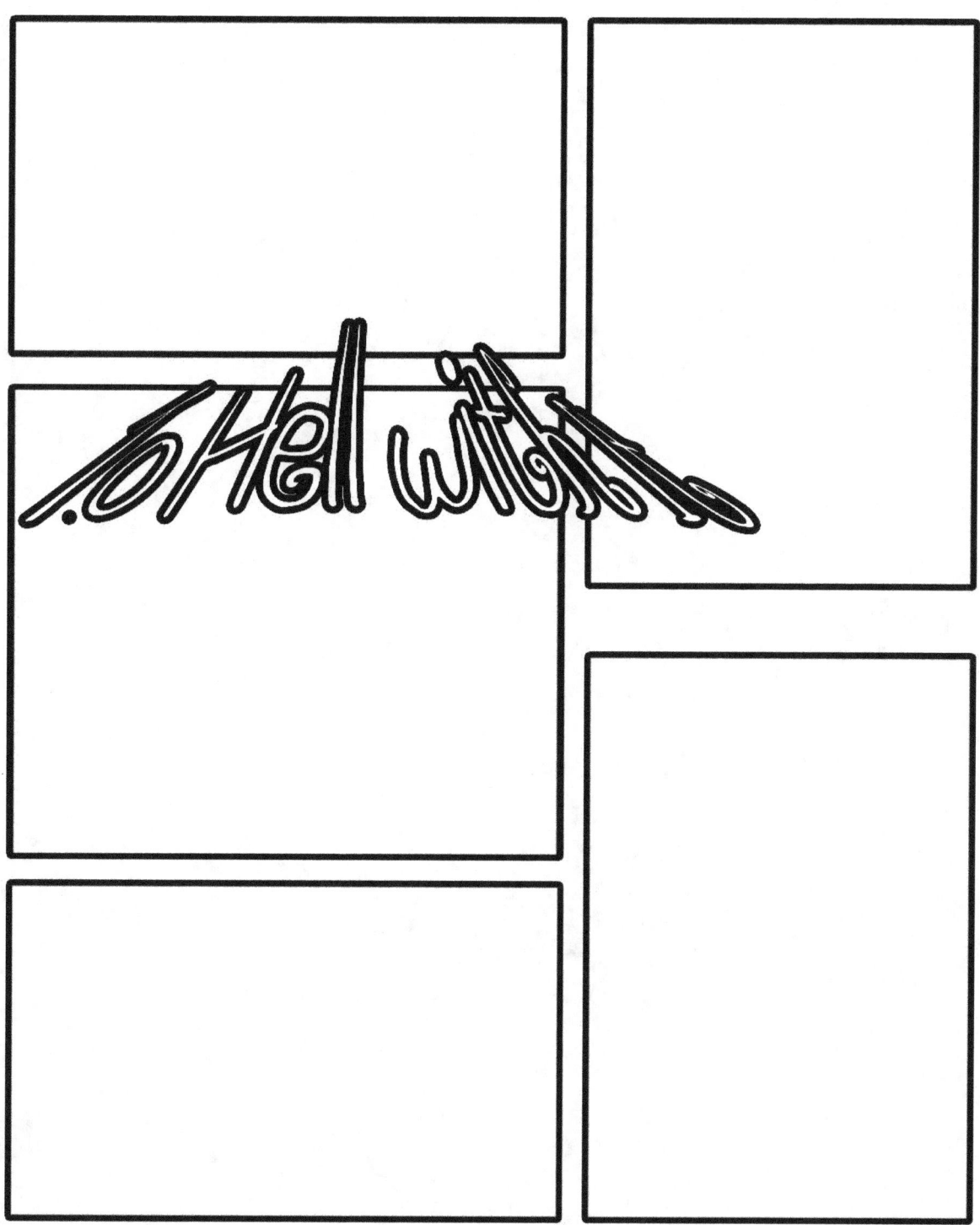

www.ingramcontent.com/pod-product-compliance
Lightning Source LLC
Chambersburg PA
CBHW081120180526
45170CB00008B/2930